RETIREMENT ISSUES, PLANS AND LIFESTYLES

INDIVIDUAL RETIREMENT ACCOUNTS

SIZE OF BALANCE ISSUES AND ENFORCEMENT OF IRS RULES

RETIREMENT ISSUES, PLANS AND LIFESTYLES

Additional books in this series can be found on Nova's website under the Series tab.

Additional e-books in this series can be found on Nova's website under the e-book tab.

RETIREMENT ISSUES, PLANS AND LIFESTYLES

INDIVIDUAL RETIREMENT ACCOUNTS

SIZE OF BALANCE ISSUES AND ENFORCEMENT OF IRS RULES

JAKE SILVA
EDITOR

nova publishers
New York

Library of Congress Cataloging-in-Publication Data

ISBN: 978-1-63482-176-6

Published by Nova Science Publishers, Inc. † New York

CONTENTS

PREFACE

This book describes IRA balances in terms of reported FMV aggregated by taxpayers; examines how IRA balances can become large; and assesses how IRS ensures that taxpayers comply with IRA tax laws.

Chapter 1 – In 2014, the federal government will forgo an estimated $17.45 billion in tax revenue from IRAs, which Congress created to ensure equitable tax treatment for those not covered by employer-sponsored retirement plans. Congress limited annual contributions to IRAs to prevent the tax-favored accumulation of unduly large balances. But concerns have been raised about whether the tax incentives encourage new or additional saving. Congress is reexamining retirement tax incentives as part of tax reform.GAO was asked to measure IRA balances and assess IRS enforcement of IRA laws.

This report (1) describes IRA balances in terms of reported FMV aggregated by taxpayers; (2) examines how IRA balances can become large; and (3) assesses how IRS ensures that taxpayers comply with IRA tax laws. To address these objectives, GAO analyzed 2011 IRS statistical data, reviewed IRS documentation and relevant literature, and interviewed government officials, financial industry stakeholders, and academics. GAO compared IRS enforcement plans and procedures with law and criteria for evaluating an enforcement program.

Chapter 2 – This is the Testimony of Scott F. Betts, Senior Vice President of National Benefits Services, LLC. Hearing on "Retirement Savings 2.0: Updating Savings Policy for the Modern Economy."

Chapter 3 – This is the Statement of Ellen E. Schultz, Author and Investigative Reporter. Hearing on "Retirement Savings 2.0: Updating Savings Policy for the Modern Economy."

In: Individual Retirement Accounts
Editor: Jake Silva
ISBN: 978-1-63482-176-6

Chapter 1

INDIVIDUAL RETIREMENT ACCOUNTS: IRS COULD BOLSTER ENFORCEMENT ON MULTIMILLION DOLLAR ACCOUNTS, BUT MORE DIRECTION FROM CONGRESS IS NEEDED*

United States Government Accountability Office

WHY GAO DID THIS STUDY

In 2014, the federal government will forgo an estimated $17.45 billion in tax revenue from IRAs, which Congress created to ensure equitable tax treatment for those not covered by employer-sponsored retirement plans. Congress limited annual contributions to IRAs to prevent the tax-favored accumulation of unduly large balances. But concerns have been raised about whether the tax incentives encourage new or additional saving. Congress is reexamining retirement tax incentives as part of tax reform.GAO was asked to measure IRA balances and assess IRS enforcement of IRA laws.

This report (1) describes IRA balances in terms of reported FMV aggregated by taxpayers; (2) examines how IRA balances can become large; and (3) assesses how IRS ensures that taxpayers comply with IRA tax laws. To

* This is an edited, reformatted and augmented version of a United States Government Accountability Office publication, No. GAO-15-16, dated October 2014.

address these objectives, GAO analyzed 2011 IRS statistical data, reviewed IRS documentation and relevant literature, and interviewed government officials, financial industry stakeholders, and academics. GAO compared IRS enforcement plans and procedures with law and criteria for evaluating an enforcement program.

WHAT GAO RECOMMENDS

Congress should consider revisiting its legislative vision for the use of IRAs. GAO makes five recommendations to IRS, including approving plans to fully compile and digitize new data on nonpublicly traded IRA assets and seeking to extend the statute of limitations for IRA noncompliance. IRS generally agreed with GAO's recommendations.

WHAT GAO FOUND

For tax year 2011 (the most recent year available), an estimated 43 million taxpayers had individual retirement accounts (IRA) with a total reported fair market value (FMV) of $5.2 trillion. As shown in the table below, few taxpayers had aggregated balances exceeding $5 million as of 2011. Generally, taxpayers with IRA balances greater than $5 million tend to have adjusted gross incomes greater than $200,000, be joint filers, and are age 65 or older. Large individual and employer contributions sustained over decades and rolled over from an employer plan would be necessary to accumulate an IRA balance of more than $5 million. There is no total statutory limit on IRA accumulations or rollovers from employer defined contribution plans.

A small number of taxpayers has accumulated larger IRA balances, likely by investing in assets unavailable to most investors—initially valued very low and offering disproportionately high potential investment returns if successful. Individuals who invest in these assets using certain types of IRAs can escape taxation on investment gains. For example, founders of companies who use IRAs to invest in nonpublicly traded shares of their newly formed companies can realize many millions of dollars in tax-favored gains on their investment if the company is successful. With no total limit on IRA accumulations, the government forgoes millions in tax revenue. The accumulation of these large IRA balances by a small number of investors stands in contrast to Congress's aim to prevent the tax-favored accumulation of balances exceeding what is needed for retirement.

Estimated Taxpayers with Individual Retirement Accounts (IRA) by Size of IRA Balance, Tax Year 2011

	Number of taxpayers			Total IRA fair market value balances (Dollars in billions)		
IRA Balance	Estimate	95% confidence interval		Estimate	95% confidence interval	
$1 million or less	42,382,192	42,094,009	42,670,375	$4,092	$4,038	$4,147
> $1 million to $2 million	502,392	470,897	533,887	674	632	717
> $2 million to $3 million	83,529	72,632	94,426	198	173	224
> $3 million to $5 million	36,171	30,811	41,531	133	114	153
> $5 million to $10 million	7,952	6,120	9,783	52	40	64
> $10 million to $25 million	791	596	985	11	8	13
> $25 million	314	115	650	81	8	225

Source: GAO analysis of IRS data. | GAO-15-16.

Notes: The taxpayer reflects a taxpaying unit including individuals as well as couples filing jointly, which may have more than one IRA owner. The IRA balance aggregates the value of all IRAs owned, including inherited IRAs.

The Internal Revenue Service (IRS) has enforcement programs covering specific aspects of IRA noncompliance, such as excess contributions and undervalued assets. As recommended by an internal task team, IRS plans to collect data identifying nonpublicly traded assets comprising IRA investments. IRS expects the data will help it identify potential IRA noncompliance. However, research on those taxpayers and IRA assets at risk will hinge on getting resources to effectively compile and analyze the additional data. IRS officials said IRA valuation cases are audit-intensive and difficult to litigate because of the subjective nature of valuation. Additionally, the 3-year statute of limitations for assessing taxes owed can pose an obstacle for IRS pursuing noncompliant activity that spans years of IRA investment.

ABBREVIATIONS

AGI	adjusted gross income
ATTI	Abusive Transactions and Technical Issues Program
AUR	Automated Underreporter Program
CIP	compliance initiative project
DB	defined benefit

DC	defined contribution
DOL	Department of Labor
ERISA	Employee Retirement Income Security Act of 1974
FMV	fair market value
IMT	Issue Management Team
IRA	individual retirement account
IRS	Internal Revenue Service
JCT	Joint Committee on Taxation
LB&I	Large Business and International Division
PwC	PricewaterhouseCoopers
S&P	Standard & Poor's
SB/SE	Small Business/Self-Employed Division
SEC	Securities and Exchange Commission
SEP	Simplified Employee Pension Plan
SIMPLE	Savings Incentive Match Plan for Employees
SOI	Statistics of Income
TE/GE	Tax-Exempt/Government Entities
TIGTA	Treasury Inspector General for Tax Administration
Treasury	Department of the Treasury
W&I	Wage and Investment Division

* * *

October 20, 2014

The Honorable Ron Wyden Chairman
Committee on Finance
United States Senate

Dear Mr. Chairman,

Enacted as part of the Employee Retirement Income Security Act of 1974 (ERISA), individual retirement accounts (IRA) are a key vehicle for individuals to save for retirement. IRAs hold about 26 percent of all retirement assets, and more than 54 million taxpayers held an estimated $5 trillion in IRAs in 2010, according to the latest published analysis by the Internal Revenue Service (IRS).[1] IRAs also are increasingly important as a way for individuals to roll over savings from pension plans. Most eligible taxpayers do not take advantage of IRAs as an opportunity to save for retirement. For example, the IRS estimated that of 145.6 million taxpayers eligible to contribute to an IRA in 2010, less than 8 percent contributed.

In 2014, tax-preferred treatment for IRAs will result in the federal government forgoing an estimated $17.45 billion in net income tax revenue, according to estimates by the Department of the Treasury (Treasury).[2] To limit the amount of federal revenue forgone and their use by higher-income individuals, IRAs are subject to a total annual contribution limit, as well as some income and other limits on eligibility. In addition, some IRA types require minimum distributions starting at age 701/2. The tax code also imposes an additional tax on excess contributions and early withdrawals. However, the tax code does not place any total limit on how much can be accumulated in an IRA.[3]

Given the potential amount of forgone revenue for the federal government—as well as questions we have raised in the past about whether tax incentives encourage new or additional saving—the ongoing debate about reforming the tax code includes reexamining the tax treatment of retirement savings.[4] Our 2005 publication, *Understanding the Tax Reform Debate*, describes long-standing criteria—economic efficiency, equity, simplicity, transparency, and administrability—that can be used to evaluate tax policy.[5] Our 2012 guide lays out a framework using these criteria to evaluate the performance of a tax expenditure, such as the beneficial tax treatment of IRAs under an income tax system.[6]

To better understand how balances accumulate in some IRAs, you asked us to review IRA account balances and IRS enforcement of IRA rules. This report (1) describes the number and types of taxpayers with IRAs and the size of IRA balances in terms of aggregate fair market value (FMV), adjusted gross income (AGI), filing status, and age; (2) examines how IRA balances can become large; and (3) assesses how IRS ensures that taxpayers comply with IRA tax laws.

To describe the number and types of taxpayers with IRAs and the size of IRA balances in terms of FMV, we analyzed individual tax data for tax year 2011 (the most recent year available) from IRS's Statistics of Income (SOI). We analyzed these data by size of IRA FMV—as reported by IRA custodians to IRS—as well as other factors, including the type of IRA, taxpayers' adjusted gross income, age, and filing status. Because SOI samples tax returns, and taxpayers may have multiple IRAs, we aggregated IRA data (including inherited IRAs as IRS data do not readily identify inherited IRAs) by tax return. Our unit of analysis was the taxpaying unit, and a tax return, such as for a married couple filing jointly, may include more than one IRA owner. Our analysis of SOI statistical data is subject to sampling errors because the SOI data set is based on a sample of tax returns as filed.[7] In addition, the data do not reflect IRS audit results. To assess the reliability of the statistical data we analyzed, we reviewed IRS documentation and interviewed agency officials familiar with the data. We determined that these data were sufficiently reliable for the purposes of this report. However, the IRS SOI sample may not provide a precise estimate of the number of taxpayers or other quantities when the number of taxpayers in a particular reporting group is very small.[8] To give perspective on what might be considered a large IRA, we developed two contribution scenarios to illustrate how much a person and an employer could have contributed given statutory limits on contributions from 1975 to 2011. We calculated hypothetical accumulations using historical stock and bond market returns and interest rates as well as what return rates would be necessary to accumulate balances of $1 million or $5 million under each contribution scenario.

To examine how IRA balances can become large, we conducted literature reviews on IRA investment strategies and held semistructured interviews with finance industry stakeholders, government officials, and academics. We selected interviewees through our literature reviews and through referrals from internal and external stakeholders for individuals with relevant legal, tax, and financial expertise. We also searched for documentary evidence of IRA investment strategies in publicly available filings with the Department of Labor (DOL) and the Securities and Exchange Commission (SEC). We could not determine how many IRAs used the strategies identified because IRS does not collect data on asset types held in IRAs. We then compared our findings from the literature reviews, interviews, and filing searches with our criteria on tax expenditures and tax policy, focusing primarily on whether the tax treatment is fair and equitable.[9]

To assess how IRS ensures that taxpayers with IRAs comply with IRA tax laws, we first developed criteria for evaluating an enforcement program on IRAs. Generally, the basis for the criteria included relevant laws, our previous work, and other organizations' work on good management practices.[10] We also shared our criteria with IRS officials. The criteria we developed are as follows:

- Enforcement programs should cover key IRA laws.
- Enforcement procedures should take into account the cumulative tax-revenue effect of an improperly valued asset that the taxpayer contributed to a plan.

- Enforcement management should collect and use data that will enable examiners to accurately weigh the noncompliance risk of potentially misreported IRA values.
- IRAs should be considered in making enforcement plans.
- Examiners should be trained to identify potential IRA noncompliance.
- IRS should collaborate with the appropriate agency on enforcing certain prohibited transactions that could lead to large, noncompliant IRAs.
- Examination management should collaborate with staff in its own service and outreach functions to help the public better understand laws related to potential IRA investment.

We then compared the criteria to documentation on IRS enforcement plans and procedures. We also collected information for the comparison from interviews with relevant IRS, Treasury, and DOL officials.

For more detail on our methodology, see appendix I.

We conducted this performance audit from June 2013 through October 2014 in accordance with generally accepted government auditing standards. Those standards require that we plan and perform the audit to obtain sufficient, appropriate evidence to provide a reasonable basis for our findings and conclusions based on our audit objectives. We believe that the evidence obtained provides a reasonable basis for our findings and conclusions based on our audit objectives.

BACKGROUND

IRAs serve dual roles by (1) providing a way for individuals not covered by a pension plan to save for retirement and (2) providing a place for retiring workers or individuals changing jobs to roll over, or transfer, their employer-sponsored pension plan balances.

IRA Types

During the past 40 years, several types of IRAs with different features for individuals and small businesses have been authorized. Two types of IRAs are geared toward individuals—each with its own federal income tax benefits:[11]

- **Traditional IRA:** Eligible individuals may make tax-deductible contributions of earned income with taxes deferred on investment earnings until distribution at retirement. If either the taxpayer or his or her spouse is covered by an employer retirement plan, the individual may be eligible for only a partial deduction or no deduction at all, depending on the taxpayer's income and filing status. Individuals may make nondeductible contributions to receive the tax deferral on investment earnings. Individuals older than 70% cannot contribute and must begin receiving required minimum distributions from these accounts. [12] Generally, distributions are taxed as ordinary income. Individuals who made nondeductible contributions to their IRAs may receive a tax-free return of those amounts. Early withdrawals before age 59%, other than for specific exceptions, are subject to a 10 percent additional income tax.
- **Roth IRA:** Enacted as part of the Taxpayer Relief Act of 1997, this type of IRA allows eligible individuals to make nondeductible contributions to these accounts but generally receive tax-free distributions.[13] Annual Roth IRA contributions are limited based on a taxpayer's income and filing status. Since January 1, 2010, conversions—where a taxpayer pays taxes deferred on balances in a traditional IRA to transfer those amounts to a Roth IRA—are no longer subject to income eligibility rules.[14] There are no age limits on contributing, and no distributions are required during the individual's lifetime. Withdrawals are generally tax-free after age 59%, as long as the individual held the account for 5 years; early distributions other than for specific exceptions are subject to an additional 10 percent income tax on earnings.

The dollar limit on all IRA contributions is adjusted annually for cost-of-living increases.[15] For 2014, the maximum contribution for all traditional and Roth IRAs in total is $5,500. Individuals age 50 and older are eligible to make additional catch-up contributions of $1,000. Taxpayers age 70% and older can contribute to a Roth IRA only. Any contribution exceeding the annual limit or made by an ineligible taxpayer is subject to a 6 percent excise tax on the amount of excess contributions.

Two other types of IRAs are intended to encourage savings sponsored through small employers:[16]

- **Simplified Employee Pension Plan (SEP) IRA:** Enacted under the Revenue Act of 1978, this type of IRA was designed with fewer regulatory requirements than traditional employer pension plans to encourage small employers to offer pension plans to their workers.[17] SEP IRAs allow employers to make tax-deductible contributions to their own and each eligible employee's accounts. SEP IRAs have higher contribution limits than other IRAs: $52,000 in 2014. Annual contributions are not mandatory, but as with pension plans, they must be based on a written allocation formula and cannot discriminate in favor of highly-compensated employees.
- **Savings Incentive Match Plan for Employees (SIMPLE) IRA:** Enacted under the Small Business Job Protection Act of 1996, SIMPLE IRAs help employers with 100 or fewer employees more easily provide a retirement savings plan to their employees.[18] In this plan, eligible employees can direct a portion of their salary, within limits, to a SIMPLE IRA and employers must either (1) match the employees' contribution up to 3 percent of the employee's compensation, or (2) make nonelective, 2 percent contributions of each employee's salary for all employees making at least $5,000 for the year. The employee salary reduction contribution limit for 2014 is $12,000.[19] Employers can elect to permit catch-up contributions, which in 2014 are limited to $2,500.

Rollovers from Employer Plans

Individuals can roll over assets from employer retirement plans into traditional or Roth IRAs.[20] Employers may sponsor two broad types of retirement plans: (1) defined benefit (DB) plans, which promise to provide benefits generally based on an employee's years of service and frequently are based on salary, regardless of the performance of the plans' investments, and (2) defined contribution (DC) plans, in which benefits are based on contributions and the performance of the investments in participants' individual accounts. Over the last three decades, employers have shifted from sponsoring DB plans to DC plans. The 401(k) plan is the predominant type of DC plan in the United States. Typically, 401(k) plans allow participants to specify the size of their contributions and direct those contributions to one or more investments among the options offered within the plan.

In passing ERISA, Congress intended to harmonize the regulation of all tax-advantaged retirement plans, including IRAs, to prevent, among other things, "[u]njustifiable differences in tax treatment of corporate owner-employees and self-employed individuals under qualified plans."[21] At the time, while DB plans were the dominant type of employer-sponsored retirement plan, Congress placed various limits on both DB and DC plans. For DB plans, benefits are limited to amounts needed to provide an annual benefit no larger than the lesser of a specific dollar amount or 100 percent of the participant's average compensation for the highest 3 consecutive calendar years.[22] For tax year 2014, the limit on the maximum annual benefit under a DB plan is $210,000. An individual receiving a lump sum distribution from a qualified plan may defer taxes by rolling the lump sum into a traditional IRA.

Whereas DB plans have a limit on total benefits, DC plans (like IRAs) have annual contribution limits but no total limit on how much an account can accumulate. For DC plans, annual contributions are limited to the lesser of a specific dollar amount or 100 percent of the participant's compensation. [23] For tax year 2014, the contribution limit on an employee's elective deferral is $17,500, and the overall contribution limit, which includes the total of all employer contributions and employee elective deferrals, is $52,000.[24] Employees age 50 and older are eligible to make additional catch-up contributions of $5,500. Employees older than age 701/2 generally can continue contributing and, if their employer plan allows, delay required minimum distributions until retirement. Rollovers from employer plans such as 401(k) plans have become the predominant source of funds into IRAs.[25] Tax-deferred balances may roll into a traditional IRA, and balances from a designated Roth account can roll directly into a Roth IRA.[26]

For employer plans, tax incentives are structured to strike a balance between encouraging employers to start and maintain voluntary, tax-qualified pension plans and ensuring that lower-income employees receive an equitable share of the tax-subsidized benefits.[27] In addition to the annual limit on employee contributions, other statutory limits include, for example, a limit on the amount of compensation ($260,000 for 2014) that can be taken into account in determining qualified pension plan contributions or benefits.[28] One important requirement for tax-qualified pension plans of private employers is that contributions or benefits be apportioned in a nondiscriminatory manner between highly compensated employees or other workers.

IRA Investments

IRA owners have wide latitude in the types of assets in which they can invest.[29] IRA owners can choose to invest in publicly traded securities or assets in custody of a financial institution or custodian. As a way to invest in a wider range of assets, albeit with higher risk, some IRA owners choose to invest in nonpublicly traded alternative assets, such as real estate and private placement stock.[30] Alternative assets may involve more direction of investment and activities by the IRA owner, limiting the typical role of the custodian.

An IRA owner choosing to directly control IRA assets or invest in alternative investments must navigate the IRA tax laws and can face additional taxes for noncompliance. An IRA owner is not permitted to engage in certain prohibited transactions with the IRA. These transactions are prohibited to prevent misuse of an IRA to benefit the owner or other disqualified persons in a way other than as a vehicle to save for retirement.[31] Such prohibited transactions specifically include, for example, borrowing money from an IRA, selling property to an IRA, using an IRA account as security for a loan, and buying property for personal use with IRA funds. If the IRA owner or beneficiary engages in a prohibited transaction, the IRA loses its status as an IRA. As a result, the account is treated as distributing all of its assets to the IRA owner at the FMV on the first day of the year in which the transaction occurred.[32] The distribution may be subject to any additional income taxes associated with an early distribution and additional excise taxes.[33]

IRA custodians are responsible for ensuring that all IRA assets (including those not publicly traded) are valued annually at their FMV and are required to report the account's FMV at year-end to IRS.[34] The FMV is the value reflecting contributions and rollovers into the IRA, distributions from the IRA, investment earnings (such as interest and dividends), and any change in the market value of assets held in the IRA. Nonpublicly traded assets do not have easily determined FMV.

IRS Enforcement and Taxpayer Service

Multiple IRS units are responsible for enforcing IRA tax laws and conducting outreach activities to increase taxpayer understanding of the laws.[35] Also, IRS and DOL share responsibility for overseeing prohibited transactions relating to IRAs. DOL defines the prohibited transactions and may grant exemptions.[36] IRS assesses additional taxes for IRAs found to engage in prohibited transactions.

Third-party reporting by IRA custodians provides information that taxpayers can use in preparing their tax returns and that IRS can use to identify noncompliant taxpayers.[37] For every IRA, the custodian is required to submit a *Form 5498 IRA Contribution Information* to IRS. The form details the IRA type (traditional, SEP, SIMPLE, or Roth), total contributions, Roth conversions, rollovers, and FMV of the account.[38] In IRA examinations, FMV may be essential in determining a plan or an IRA's compliance with the law, such as whether the contribution value causes a taxpayer to violate contribution limits. Custodians are also to report on Form 5498 whether a taxpayer is subject to required minimum distributions for the coming year; custodians are not required to report the minimum amount calculated for each account. The custodian is also required to submit a *Form 1099-R Distributions From Pensions, Annuities, Retirement or Profit-Sharing Plans, IRAs, Insurance Contracts, etc.,* each year that indicates an IRA withdrawal took place and details the total distributions from the account during the calendar year. Form 1099- R also provides information about the IRA distributions, such as whether the distributions were taken before age 591/2.[39]

The IRS Wage and Investment division operates automated enforcement programs that check taxpayer reporting of IRA transactions. The math error program checks tax returns for conspicuous taxpayer errors as tax returns are processed.[40] The automated underreporter program (AUR) identifies noncompliance with certain IRA deduction and distribution rules by matching custodians' Form 5498 and Form 1099-R information returns with taxpayers' income tax returns. AUR may ask taxpayers for additional information to reconcile discrepancies. Some AUR cases may be handled as correspondence examinations, while other IRA compliance issues, such as those with large asset values, may be referred for field examination.[41]

The IRS Small Business/Self-Employed (SB/SE) division conducts field examinations targeting more complex individual tax returns. Field examinations are IRS's most costly form of examination. Figure 1 shows SB/SE's process for examining returns.

Whereas SB/SE examines individual tax returns, the IRS Tax Exempt/Government Entities division (TE/GE) has jurisdiction over employee plans (including employer-sponsored SEP and SIMPLE IRA plans) and requirements for rollovers from qualified employer plans into IRAs. If TE/GE examiners discover an individual tax issue, they may refer it to other examination offices, including SB/SE.

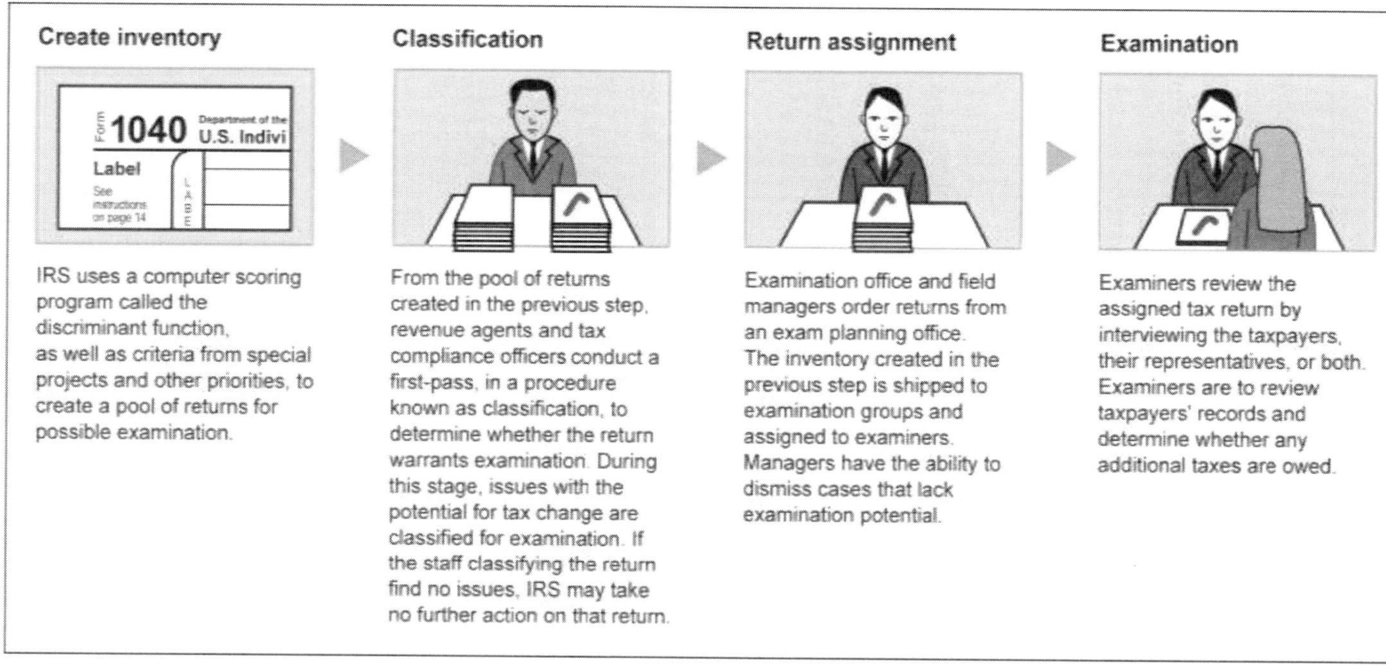

Source: GAO analysis of IRS information. | GAO-15-16.

Figure 1. Small Business/Self-Employed Examination Process.

IRS service activities aim to increase taxpayer understanding of and improve compliance with tax obligations, including IRA requirements, as well as deliver clear and focused outreach communications and education programs to assist taxpayer understanding of tax responsibilities and awareness of changing tax laws. IRS *Publication 590 Individual Retirement Arrangements (IRAs)* (*Publication 590*) explains the requirements that taxpayers are to follow in contributing to, and receiving distributions from, traditional, Roth, and SIMPLE IRAs.[42]

FEW TAXPAYERS HAD REPORTED IRA BALANCES GREATER THAN $5 MILLION

Most Taxpayers with IRAs Have IRA Balances of $1 Million or Less

Of the 145 million married couples and individuals who filed individual income tax returns for tax year 2011, an estimated 43 million, or 30 percent, had IRAs with an estimated total balance—in terms of FMV reported by custodians—of $5.2 trillion at the end of 2011.[43] About 99 percent of those taxpayers had aggregate IRA balances of $1 million or less and accounted for around 78 percent of the total balance. The median accumulated IRA balance for this group was around $34,000. Taxpayers with aggregated IRA balances exceeding $1 million, around 600,000 taxpayers, accounted for about 22 percent of total balance and had a median of around $1.4 million.

As seen in tables 1 and 2, less than 0.1 percent of taxpayers (about 6,000 to 10,000 taxpayers) had aggregated IRA balances greater than $5 million to $10 million but accounted for about 1 percent of the total balance. From around 700 to more than 1,000 taxpayers with IRA balances more than $10 million accounted for about 2 percent of the total balance.[44] A number of taxpayers had IRA balances exceeding $25 million though our estimates varied widely from around 115 to more than 600 taxpayers. Some of these taxpayers had very large aggregated balances (see appendix III, table 10 for estimated median IRA balances by size of IRA balance and their associated ranges).[45]

Table 1. Estimated Number and Percent of Taxpayers with Individual Retirement Accounts (IRA) by Size of IRA Balance, Tax Year 2011

IRA Balance	Estimated number of taxpayers	95% confidence interval		Estimated percent of taxpayers with IRAs	95% confidenc e interval	
Total taxpayers with IRAs	43,013,341	42,725,706	43,300,975	100	100	100
$1 million or less	42,382,192	42,094,009	42,670,375	98.5	98.5	98.6
> $1 million to $2 million	502,392	470,897	533,887	1.2	1.1	1.2
> $2 million to $3 million	83,529	72,632	94,426	0.2	0.2	0.2
> $3 million to $5 million	36,171	30,811	41,531	0.1	0.1	0.1
> $5 million to $10 million	7,952	6,120	9,783	<0.1	<0.1	<0.1
> $10 million to $25 million	791	596	985	<0.1	<0.1	<0.1
> $25 million	314	115	650	<0.1	<0.1	<0.1

Source: GAO analysis of IRS data from Forms 1040, U.S. Individual Income Tax Returns and Forms 5498 IRA Contribution Information. | GAO-15-16.

Notes: The taxpayer, as a taxpaying unit, may have more than one IRA owner. The IRA balance is the aggregate value for all IRAs (including inherited IRAs) owned by the taxpayer. We assumed all blank IRA fair market values are zero; the blank values could affect these estimates considerably. See appendix I for more details. Percentages may not total 100 percent due to rounding.

Table 2. Estimated Total and Percent of Individual Retirement Account (IRA) Fair Market Value Balances by Size of IRA Balance, Tax Year 2011

IRA Balance	Estimated total IRA balances ($ billions)	95% confidence interval		Estimated percent of total IRA balances	95% confidence interval	
Total taxpayers with IRAs	5,241	5,083	5,399	100	100	100
$1 Million or less	4,092	4,038	4,147	78.1	75.8	80.3
> $1 Million to $2 million	674	632	717	12.9	12.1	13.7
> $2 million to $3 million	198	173	224	3.8	3.3	4.3
> $3 million to $5 million	133	114	153	2.5	2.2	2.9
> $5 million to $10 million	52	40	64	1.0	0.8	1.2
> $10 million to $25 million	11	8	13	0.2	0.2	0.3
> $25 million	81	8	225	1.5	<0.2	4.2

Source: GAO analysis of IRS data from Forms 1040, U.S. Individual Income Tax Returns and Forms 5498 IRA Contribution Information.| GAO-15-16.

Notes: The taxpayer, as a taxpaying unit, may have more than one IRA owner.

The IRA balance is the aggregate value for all IRAs (including inherited IRAs) owned by the taxpayer. We assumed the blank IRA fair market values are zero; the blank values could affect these estimates considerably. See appendix I for details. Percentage may not total 100 percent due to rounding.

To characterize taxpayers with IRAs by IRA type, adjusted gross income (AGI), filing status, and age, we compare two subgroups of taxpayers— those with IRA balances of $1 million or less, which comprised 99 percent of all taxpayers with IRAs, and those with IRA balances of more than $5 million. We do not report on taxpayers with IRA balances greater than $1 million to $5 million to avoid disclosure of taxpayer information.

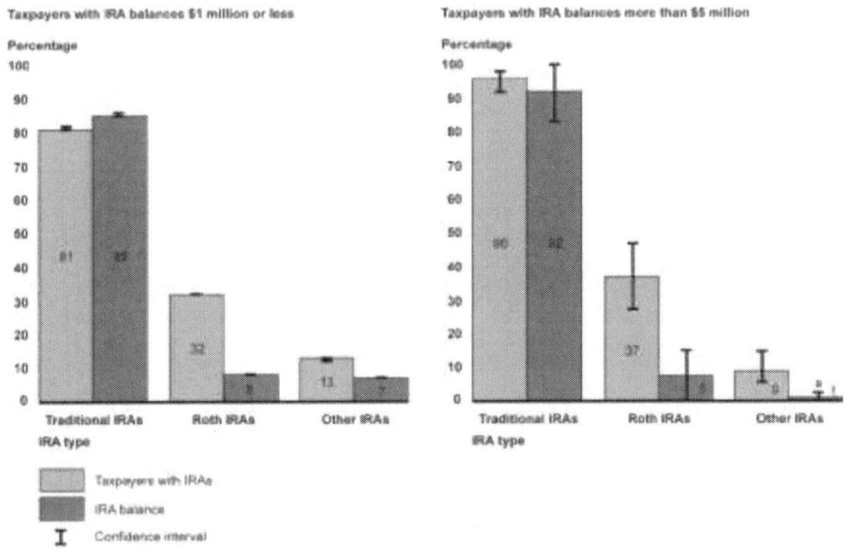

Source: GAO analysis of IRS data. | GAO-15-16.

Notes: As taxpayers can have more than one type of IRA, the type of IRAs do not sum to 100 percent. All percent estimates have margins of error at the 95 percent confidence level or plus or minus 10 percent points or less. We assumed all the blank IRA fair market values are zeros; the blank values could affect our estimates considerably. See appendix I for more details.

[a]The distributions for these estimates are so skewed that the usual estimation methods do not produce an accurate lower bound.

Figure 2. Estimated Percent of Taxpayers with Individual Retirement Account (IRA) Balances of $1 Million or Less and More Than $5 Million and Percent of IRA Balance, by IRA Type, Tax Year 2011.

Taxpayers held about 87 percent of the total balance in traditional IRAs, around $4.4 trillion to $4.7 trillion, while the proportion of total balance held in Roth IRAs was 7 percent, around $359 billion to $378 billion. Those held in other employer-sponsored SEP and SIMPLE IRAs, around 6 percent, accounted for the remaining value. Figure 2 shows a breakdown of IRA types by taxpayers with IRA balances of $1 million or less and those with balances of more than $5 million.

Taxpayers with IRA Balances Exceeding $5 Million Have Higher AGI

For those taxpayers with IRA balances of $1 million or less, most (around 90 percent) have AGI of $200,000 or less.[46] For those with IRA balances of more than $5 million, most (about 90 percent) have AGI greater than $200,000. However our estimates for this subgroup are imprecise as seen in the wide confidence intervals in figure 3.

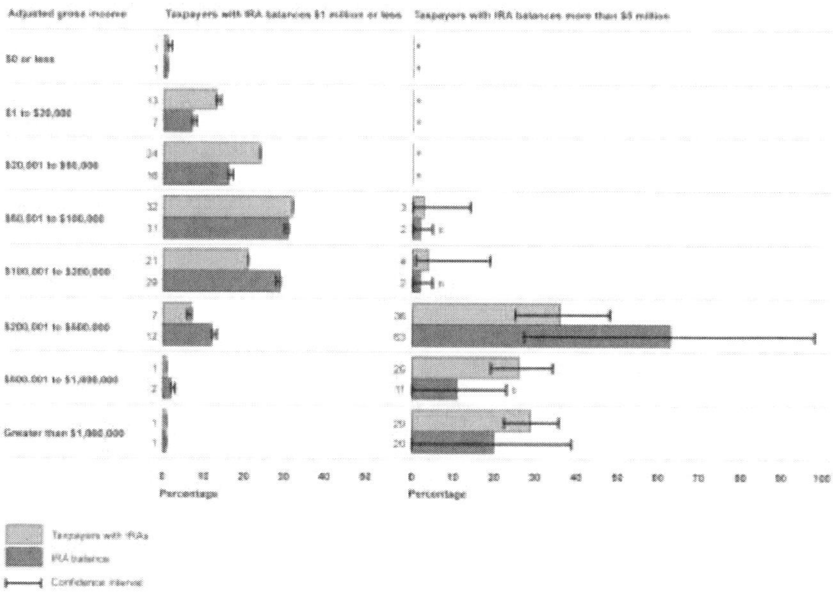

Source: GAO analysis of IRS data. | GAO-15-16.

Notes: See appendix III, tables 11 and 12 for the 95th percent confidence intervals associated with these estimates.

We assumed all the blank IRA fair market values are zeros; the blank values could affect our estimates considerably. See appendix I for details.

[a]Estimates suppressed due to small cell counts.

[b]The distributions for these estimates are so skewed that the usual estimation methods do not produce an accurate lower bound.

Figure 3. Estimated Percent of Taxpayers with Individual Retirement Account (IRA) Balances of $1 Million or Less and More Than $5 Million and IRA Balances, by Adjusted Gross Income, Tax Year 2011.

Taxpayers with IRA Balances Greater than $5 Million Tend to be Joint Filers and Age 65 or Older

Joint filers comprised a larger proportion of taxpayers with IRA balances greater than $5 million in comparison to those with IRA balances of $1 million or less. Joint filers also accounted for a larger share of the IRA balance with about 90 percent of the IRA balance for those with balances more than $5 million, as shown in figure 4.

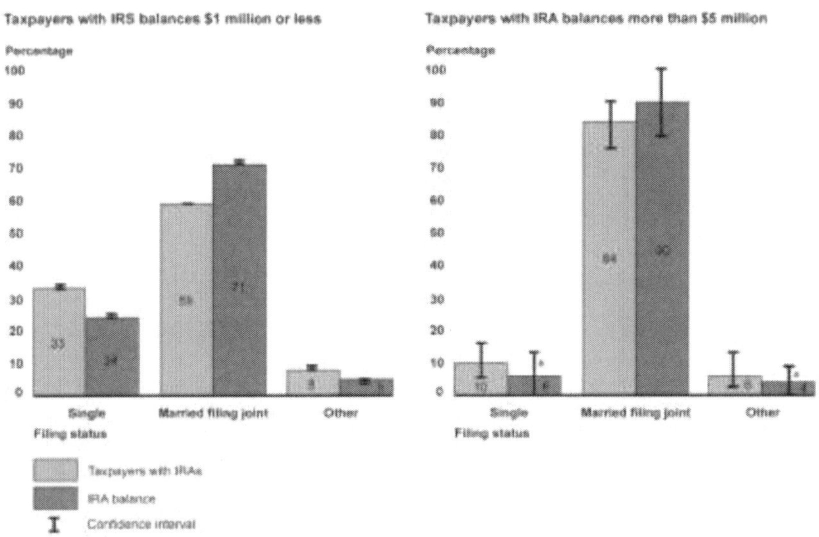

Source: GAO analysis of IRS data. | GAO-15-16.

Notes: All percent estimates have margins of error at the 95 percent confidence level or plus or minus 11 percent points or less. We assumed all the blank IRA fair market values are zeros; the blank values could affect our estimates considerably. See appendix I for details.

[a]The distributions for these estimates are so skewed that the usual estimation methods do not produce an accurate lower bound.

Figure 4. Estimated Percent of Taxpayers with Individual Retirement Account (IRA) Balances of $1 Million or Less and More Than $5 Million by Filing Status, Tax Year 2011.

Those who are age 65 and older—and have had more years to accumulate funds in IRAs—comprised at least 86 percent of taxpayers with balances greater than $5 million and about 90 percent of the total IRA balance for the group. This age group comprised a smaller percent, about 27, of taxpayers with balances of $1 million or less, but has a disproportionate share of the total IRA balance for the group, as shown in figure 5.

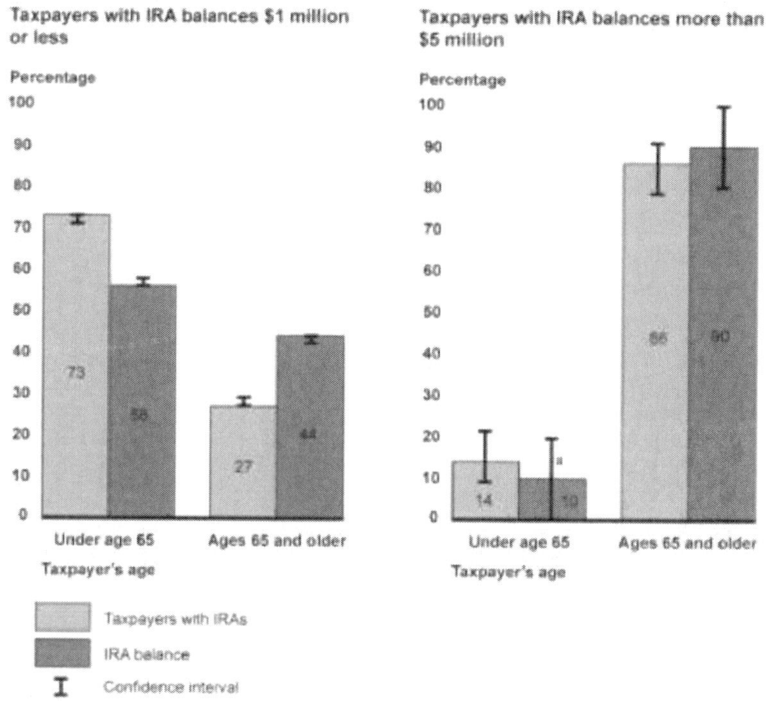

Source: GAO analysis of IRS data. | GAO-15-16.

Notes: Taxpayers were classified in the age 65 and older group if the filer, spouse, or both were age 65 or older. All percent estimates have margins of error at the 95 percent confidence level or plus or minus 10 percent points or less.

We assumed all the blank IRA fair market values are zeros; the blank values could affect our estimates considerably. See appendix I for details.

[a]The distributions for these estimates are so skewed that the usual estimation methods do not produce an accurate lower bound.

Figure 5. Estimated Percent of Taxpayers Age 65 or Older by Individual Retirement Account (IRA) Balances of $1 Million or Less and More Than $5 Million, Tax Year 2011.

IRA Balances Greater Than $5 Million Could Be Considered Large Based on What Individuals Typically Contribute

While there is no total limit on IRA or DC plan accumulations, scenarios illustrating the maximum annual contributions by an individual and employer over time can shed light on what could be considered a large IRA (see appendix I for the statutory annual contributions limits and more detailed scenario descriptions).[47] Table 3 illustrates total contributions by an individual assuming (1) maximum contributions every year since IRAs were created under ERISA, and (2) maximum employer and employee contributions since 401(k) plans were created.[48] These scenarios represent the upper bounds on allowable contributions and do not represent how much individuals and employers typically contribute. Some may not have sufficient income to even approach the employee limit or might not have an employer able or willing to provide additional contributions up to the maximum combined employee plus employer limit. For 2011, the limit for combined employer-employee contributions, (including catch-up contributions for those who are age 50 and older) totaled $54,500, with the employee contribution limit (also including catchup contributions) being $22,000. Few, if any, individuals would sustain maximum contributions for more than three decades, given that in practice, few individuals contribute the maximum to an IRA or employer DC plan in any given year. Further, few, if any, individuals would be employed by employers who made matching and additional contributions for more than three decades at a level high enough to reach the combined employee plus employer limit. Our previous work estimated that only one-tenth of 1 percent of plan participants had contributions at or above the combined employer-employee contribution limit for 2010.[49]

Nonetheless, to illustrate possible accumulations under these upper bounds for contributions, the scenarios shown in table 3 assume all contributions are invested in a broad stock market index—specifically, the Standard & Poor's (S&P) 500—and are not intended to represent how individuals typically invest. We also looked at other illustrative investment allocations, shown in appendix I.

The scenarios do not reflect any withdrawals or investment fees. As shown in table 3, it would take double-digit rates of return—in excess of the S&P 500 return over the period—to achieve a balance of $1 million or more assuming an individual made only IRA contributions.

Accounting for the maximum possible combined employer-employee contributions and no withdrawals, the DC plan scenario with investment sustained over more than three decades could accumulate an individual account balance of more than $5 million; however, as already noted, such a level of contributions is rare, and such a sustained level is improbable. Moreover, an accumulation of more than $5 million looks large in comparison to what can be substantial rollovers of lump sum payouts from an employer DB plan.[50]

Table 3. Rates of Return Needed to Accumulate Individual Retirement Account (IRA) Balances of $1 million or $5 Million under Two Illustrative Contribution Scenarios, 1975-2011

Scenario	Total contributions	Balance invested in S&P 500 portfolio Geometric mean Dollar-weighted	S&P 500 rate of return [a]		Dollar-weighted rate of return to accumulate $1 million [a]	Dollar-weightedrate of return to accumulate $5 million [a]
			Geometric mean	Dollar-weighted		
Maximum IRA contributions (1975-2011) [b]	$99,500	$729,508	11.6%	10.3%	11.6%	18.0%
Maximum combined employer-employee DC contributions (1980-2011) [c]	$1,185,350	$7,268,906	11.1%	9.8%	N/A [d]	8.0%

Source: GAO analysis based on statutory contribution limits | GAO-15-16.

Notes: All scenarios reflect contributions by an individual with catch-up contributions beginning in 2002. Scenario results do not reflect investment or administrative fees and expenses. Likewise, the scenarios do not reflect any withdrawals or employer plan loans over the period. The contributions and returns reported above are for the specific time periods of 1975-2011 for IRA accounts and 1980- 2011 for DC accounts. For the maximum combined employer-employee contribution scenario, we looked at a range of possible asset allocations in addition to the one shown in table 3 of a 100- percent investment in the S&P 500. As shown in appendix 1, ending balances of the additional scenarios ranged from $7.1 million for a 100-percent bond allocation to a high of $8.6 million for a glide path allocation starting at 70 percent invested in the S&P 500 and ending with 30 percent invested in the S&P 500. We also calculated the DC contribution scenario with the investment returns equal to historical interest rates reported by the Social Security trustees for special issue government-bonds as a proxy for a safer investment strategy, which resulted in an ending balance of $3.4 million.

[a]The S&P 500 rate of return is calculated as the geometric mean (sometimes referred to as the compounded annual growth rate) on a time-weighted basis, which means that each year's rate of return receives equal weighting in calculating the mean. We calculated the dollar-weighted return, which takes into account the intersection of the timing of cash flows into or out of the account and the timing of the investment returns. For example, because new money is being contributed to the account every year, a rate of return in a later year is more important than a rate of return in an earlier year because more money is at stake in the later years. The dollar-weighted annual rate of return adjusts for this and thereby measures the actual performance of the account under the given investment strategy. For more information on alternative return measures, see GAO, *Pension Plan Valuation: Views on Using Multiple Measures to Offer a More Complete Financial Picture*, GAO-14-264 (Washington, D.C.: Sept. 30, 2014.)

[b]The IRA scenario reflects maximum allowable contributions to a traditional IRA. For a Roth IRA, the maximum contributions for 1998 to 2011 would be $57,000.

[c]This scenario reflects the upper bound on contributions to a single employer DC plan. Our prior work has shown that about one-tenth of one percent of DC plan participants contributed at or above the combined employer-employee contribution limit for 2010.

[d] N/A = not applicable. Contributions alone accumulated from 1980 to 2011 are more than $1 million.

Nonetheless, to illustrate possible accumulations under these upper bounds for contributions, the scenarios shown in table 3 assume all contributions are invested in a broad stock market index—specifically, the Standard & Poor's (S&P) 500—and are not intended to represent how individuals typically invest. We also looked at other illustrative investment allocations, shown in appendix I.

The scenarios do not reflect any withdrawals or investment fees. As shown in table 3 above, it would take double-digit rates of return—in excess of the S&P 500 return over the period—to achieve a balance of $1 million or more assuming an individual made only IRA contributions.

Accounting for the maximum possible combined employer-employee contributions and no withdrawals, the DC plan scenario with investment sustained over more than three decades could accumulate an individual account balance of more than $5 million; however, as already noted, such a level of contributions is rare, and such a sustained level is improbable. Moreover, an accumulation of more than $5 million looks large in comparison to what can be substantial rollovers of lump sum payouts from an employer DB plan.[50]

For 2011, the maximum lump sum payable to a 65-year-old DB participant would have ranged from $2.3 million to $2.6 million, depending on the interest rate factors used in the lump sum calculations.

Finally, as discussed above, we found few taxpayers (including married couples filing jointly) with IRA balances greater than $5 million. For all of these reasons, one could consider an IRA balance accumulated by one individual greater than $5 million to be large.

Historically, IRS has collected annual FMV as reported by custodians for each IRA annually but no data on what type of assets are held in IRAs. 51 As a result, we could not describe the composition of assets held in IRAs using the available IRS SOI data.[52]

IRS officials pointed out that an individual may have a larger IRA balance by inheriting a large IRA. The IRS IRA data do not readily identify inherited IRAs, so we could not describe how many taxpayers had inherited IRA balances as of 2011.[53]

Alternate Strategies Are Likely the Cause of Large IRA Balances That Congress May Not Have Intended

Investments with Low Initial Values Not Available to Most Investors Help a Small Number of Individuals Accumulate Large IRA Balances

Our interviews with industry stakeholders and review of publicly available filings with the SEC and DOL indicate that a small number of individuals with access to certain types of nonpublicly traded shares in companies or a particular type of partnership interest, as shown in table 4, can generate IRA balances far exceeding $10 million. This is in contrast to the vast majority of IRA owners with balances well under $1 million. Although IRS data at present do not provide information on the investment strategies of IRA owners or the assets in their accounts, we found that an IRA owner would need to participate in a DC plan and sustain large contributions over decades to generate an IRA greater than $5 million. As we have previously found, IRA owners face many challenges in trying to accumulate even modest retirement savings, such as the pressure to draw down their savings for nonretirement expenses like purchasing a home or paying college tuition for their children or medical bills.[54] This is a strong indicator that the individuals able to accumulate such large balances have not done so through steady contributions and investments in publicly traded stocks, bonds, and mutual funds. Instead, these individuals likely use alternate strategies involving investments not available to most taxpayers. In addition to access, to generate a large IRA, investments must have a low initial value and the potential for unusually high investment returns. The low initial value of these investments: (1) allows the individual to purchase a quantity within IRA contribution limits sufficient to generate tens of millions of dollars if the investments are successful; and (2) protects the individual against financial loss, given the increased likelihood that these investments end up worthless. For example, according to SEC documents, the founders of one prominent technology company issued nonpublicly traded shares in the newly created company for an initial value, or par value, of $0.000001 per share.[55]

Table 4. Investments That Can Generate Tens of Millions of Dollars in a Tax-Favored Retirement Account

Nonpublicly traded shares	May be issued by the founders of a new company for a very low initial price. They may also be created for an existing company whose shares are taken off public stock exchanges for instance when the company is taken private by a group of insiders or outside investors, such as private equity firms. According to industry stakeholders, private equity funds sometimes reorganize the existing shares of companies they purchase into multiple share classes, some of which have a low initial value and higher risk than other share classes.
Partnership interests	Can be similar to shares and are issued by companies that operate as partnerships. Partnerships typically grant two types of partnership interests: I. Capital interests to outside investors, known as limited partners, generally in exchange for cash investments in the partnership. II. Profits interests to key employees in exchange for services, ideas, and expertise that benefit the partnership. In some cases, a profits interest is also referred to as a carried interest.

Source: GAO analysis of IRS guidance and industry publications. | GAO-15-16.

Note: The initial value of a capital interest is higher than that of profits interest because it reflects the outside investors' cash investment in a fund. The holder of a capital interest has a right to get any of his or her remaining initial investment back in the event the fund is unsuccessful. However, the holder of a profits interest has a right only to future profits generated by the fund if it is a success.

Nonpublicly traded shares and partnership interests can generally be accessed directly by only a small number of individuals, in part because all offers and sales of securities must be registered under the Securities Act of 1933, unless an exemption from registration is available. The most commonly used exemption limits the investors who can purchase securities in the offering to accredited investors and "sophisticated" investors who are able to evaluate the risks and merits of the investment and bear its economic risk.[56] Even among this select group, only a small number of individuals can use nonpublicly traded shares and partnership interests to generate a large IRA. For example, only the founders of successful companies and some of their initial employees and investors have access to nonpublicly traded shares issued at the creation of the company, at which time these shares can be valued at less than $0.01 apiece. Given the risks associated with starting new companies, most founders are unlikely to see their initial investment grow to a balance of tens of millions. However, founders of successful companies may accumulate large returns disproportionate to the amount they initially paid for shares in their own company.

Most investors are unlikely to have access to these investments when their value is low enough to accumulate such disproportionate investment returns. This is because few investors are likely to be founders of companies or key employees in private equity firms and hedge funds. However, some individuals who do not meet the requirements to invest directly in private equity funds and hedge funds may still be able to invest in them indirectly if they are participants in large public or private sector DB plans. We found in 2012 that an increasing percentage of large DB plans have invested in private equity funds and hedge funds in recent years.[57] Still, because pension benefits from such plans are generally set based on a participant's salary and years of service, unusually high returns from such investments are unlikely to result in greater pension plan benefits.[58]

Accumulating Nonpublicly Traded Shares in an IRA

According to a number of industry stakeholders, individuals may in some cases purchase nonpublicly traded shares using funds they accumulated in an IRA through contributions and rollovers from employer-sponsored plans. Figure 6 demonstrates an instance in which, according to SEC documents, one of the founders of a successful technology company used a Roth IRA to purchase at least 4 million nonpublicly traded shares of his newly created company. [59] For an example of how nonpublicly traded shares can generate a large IRA balance for the founder of a successful company based on this instance, see appendix IV.

Similarly, employees of private equity firms may have access to nonpublicly traded shares in companies the fund purchases, referred to as portfolio companies. In some cases, after taking the existing shares of a portfolio company off public stock exchanges, the private equity firm will restructure them into multiple share classes.[60]

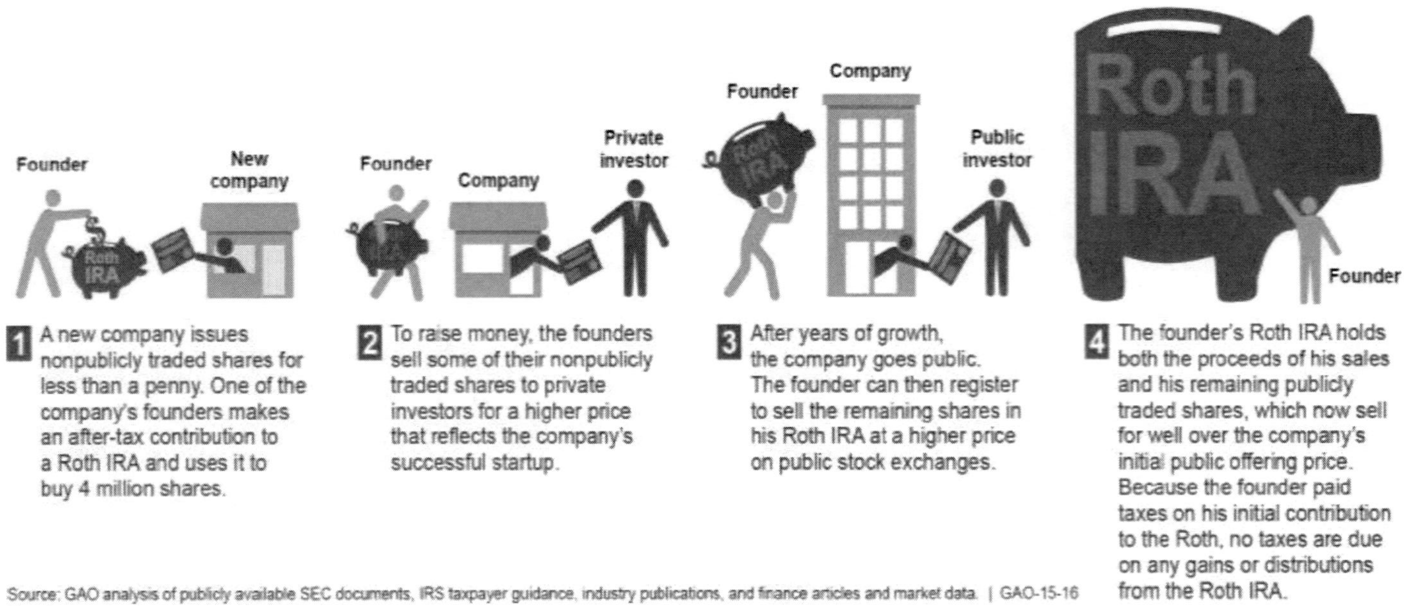

Figure 6. For a Modest Initial Investment, Nonpublicly Traded Shares Can Generate a Large IRA.

In what one industry stakeholder referred to as the "cheap stock model," these share classes include a preferred share class with a higher initial value and a riskier common share class with a lower initial value.[61] As with the nonpublicly traded shares issued by company founders, individuals may be able to purchase a quantity of the riskier share class in an IRA within contribution limits sufficient to produce substantial investment returns if the portfolio company is later sold for a sizeable profit.

According to five industry stakeholders who advise them, private equity firms can use very aggressive ratios to split the value of portfolio companies between share classes.[62] According to one industry stakeholder, the use of an aggressive ratio can result in a risky share class with a liquidation value as low as zero.[63] Although risky, these shares can increase in value very quickly, suggesting to some that their initial value may have been inappropriate. For example, in one publicly reported private equity transaction, employees of the private equity firm used their IRAs to purchase about $25,000 worth of low-valued, nonpublicly traded shares the fund created for a portfolio company. The shares were worth nearly $14 million when the private equity firm brought the portfolio company back onto public stock exchanges less than 2 years later. The employees eventually sold their shares for more than $23 million, realizing more than 1,000 times their initial investment.[64]

However, one industry stakeholder who advises private equity firms said it would be difficult for IRS to prove these shares were inappropriately valued, because, for each risky share the employees purchased, they also purchased a share from a less risky higher-priced share class. Taken together, these shares may more accurately reflect the portfolio company's value.

Generating Large IRAs through a Profits Interest (Carried Interest)

Carried interest is another means by which key employees of private equity firms and hedge funds can generate large IRA balances.[65] According to one industry stakeholder who advises wealthy clients, including key employees of private equity firms, access to profits interests was likely the chief determinant of an individual's ability to accumulate a large IRA balance. He added that the rest of his clients, even those whose wealth surpasses $100 million, were unlikely to have an IRA exceeding $5 million because of the IRA contribution limits. The share of profits paid by outside investors, known as limited partners, to the general partner as a performance fee is referred to as the general partner's carried interest in a fund.

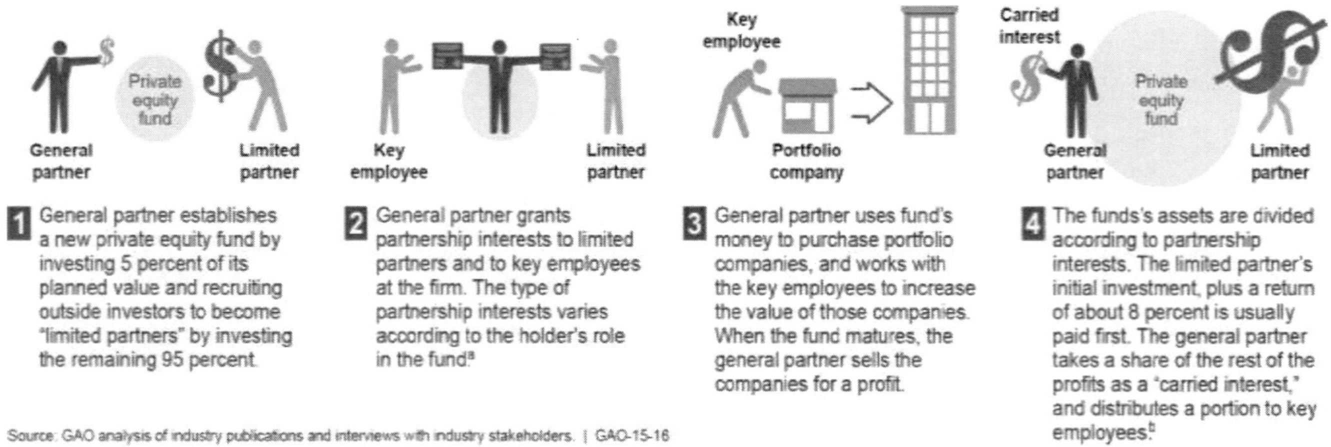

Source: GAO analysis of industry publications and interviews with industry stakeholders. | GAO-15-16

Note: Terms vary for funds offered by private equity firms and hedge funds. For example, the amount of capital contributed by the general partner and the timing for distributing profits may vary by fund. This figure does not take into account other fees charged by private equity firms and hedge funds such as management fees charged to outside investors. Industry stakeholders refer to the "two and twenty" fee structure as a guideline. This structure consists of a 2 percent management fee and a 20 percent performance fee called carried interest charged to outside investors.

[a]Outside investors get capital interests in exchange for their investment in the fund. Capital interests give outside investors a right to profits generated by the fund. Profits distributed to a capital interest are generally proportionate to the amount invested, less fees and expenses. Key employees, on the other hand, get profits interests in exchange for their ideas, expertise, and work to make the fund successful. Profits interests give key employees a right to profits generated by the fund if the fund is a success. But profits interests do not give key employees a right to any of the initial capital used to start the fund.

Because profits interests represent an investment of effort and expertise rather than money, their initial purchase price can be low, making profits interests uniquely suited to the contribution limits of tax-favored retirement accounts. The low purchase price means that returns from a profits interest can be substantially disproportionate to the money needed to purchase them, and consequently much higher than other types of investments.

[b]The general partner usually takes 20 percent of a successful fund's profits as a carried interest, although this amount is negotiated with outside investors and can vary.

Figure 7. General Partners Grant Partnership Interests in Their Investment Funds.

The general partner typically distributes a portion of this fee, referred to as an investment fund's "carry," to a few key employees by first granting them a profits interest in the fund (see fig. 7).

Source: GAO analysis of publicly available IRS guidance, industry publications, and interviews with stakeholders. | GAO-15-16.

[a]Individuals covered by employer-sponsored plans may deduct only a portion of contributions to a traditional IRA from their taxable income, depending on their income and filing status. In some instances, contributions to a traditional 401(k) account may exceed the participant's elective deferral limit but contributions may not exceed the lesser of 100 percent of the participant's compensation or an overall contribution limit.

[b]Qualified distributions from a Roth IRA that meet certain requirements are generally tax free. To be considered qualified, the IRA owner must, among other things, hold his or her investments for at least 5 years and reach age 591/2 before taking a distribution.

Figure 8. Profits Interest Can Be Held in an IRA or a Defined Contribution Plan.

A profits interest has the potential to provide a key employee investment returns that are disproportionate to his or her invested capital if the fund is a success, according to six industry stakeholders who represent private equity firms and hedge funds or advise private equity professionals. If, on the other hand, a fund does not generate a minimum rate of return for its outside investors, profits interests may expire without generating any money for the key employee. For an example of how carried interest can generate a large IRA balance, see appendix IV.

Profits interests in a private equity fund or hedge fund can have a low initial value because they do not necessarily represent a cash investment to the fund by key employees. Instead, they represent an agreement that key employees will provide expertise, ideas, and work to make the fund a success in exchange for a share of the profits from the fund. IRS provided guidance on treatment for the receipt of a profits interest for services, saying that the grant of a profits interest is generally not a taxable event.[66] Some industry stakeholders may have taken this to mean that profits interests can have an initial value of as low as $0.00, referred to as a liquidation value.

As with nonpublicly traded shares, key employees at private equity firms and hedge funds may use IRAs to purchase profits interests from the general partner. According to an industry stakeholder who advises private equity professionals in estate planning, key employees may first accumulate profits interests in a DC plan, such as a 401(k) or profit sharing plan, then subsequently roll over the assets of their employer-based account into an IRA (see fig. 8). A rollover to an IRA can include both cash and noncash assets, such as a profits interest that is not done yielding distributions of carried interest. According to DOL officials, ERISA does not necessarily prohibit an employer from contributing a profits interest to the DC plan of its employees, although Internal Revenue Code requirements administered by IRS may restrict or regulate these types of transactions.[67]

Alternate Strategies Raise Concerns but Are Difficult for IRS to Address

A number of industry stakeholders we interviewed expressed concerns that individuals who invest in nonpublicly traded shares or profits interests using IRAs and DC plans may undervalue these assets, thus substantially increasing their tax benefits. According to one industry stakeholder who advises clients on using IRAs to invest in alternative assets, individuals can manipulate contribution limits by grossly undervaluing investments at the time the individual uses an IRA to purchase them. Two industry stakeholders who advise wealthy clients or who research carried interest arrangements told us that IRA balances exceeding $10 million are a strong indication that assets may have been inappropriately valued. For example, company founders may have extensive knowledge of a company's value based on its future assets and liabilities.

It is often difficult for IRS to pursue cases of potential abuse based on inappropriately valued assets. First, in response to a congressional inquiry, IRS said it generally requires individuals to assess the FMV of assets in IRAs rather than use a liquidation value or other valuation method.[68] However, IRS guidance implies that individuals can use the liquidation value of a profits interest for certain tax purposes. One industry stakeholder also noted that individuals can use case law to support very low valuations of nonpublicly traded shares and profits interests.[69] Second, according to IRS officials, valuation can be subjective and IRS may expend resources and ultimately conclude that the taxpayer's valuation is reasonable. Third, the statute of limitations for IRS to pursue cases is generally only 3 years, which poses certain obstacles to pursuing noncompliant activity that spans years of IRA investment.[70] For example, as we have previously found, the long-term nature of private equity investment requires lengthy financial commitments and delayed financial returns. A private equity fund may not begin making profits for 4 or more years.[71] For examples of the time that may in some cases be needed to realize disproportionately large investment returns from such investments, see appendix IV.

Identifying Carried Interest in DC Plans and IRAs Is Difficult

Due to a lack of information in publicly available filings by private equity firms and hedge funds, we could not determine the extent to which key employees use DC plans or IRAs to invest in profits interests and thus shelter their portion of the general partner's carried interest from taxation. However, one industry stakeholder who values carried interest arrangements told us that he has been asked in one or two cases to value carried interest held in a profit sharing plan. We could not determine from publicly available filings with SEC and DOL if private equity firms and hedge funds enable key employees to invest in profits interests using DC plans.[72] Of the 60 private equity firms and hedge funds we reviewed, about half did not include in their filings with DOL a description of the assets held in their employer-sponsored plans.[73]

Of the filings that did include a description of assets held in the employer-sponsored plan, we found four hedge funds and one private equity firm whose employees were substantially invested in their employer's investment funds (see sidebar). However, we could not determine if these were investments in profits interests that would yield disproportionately large investment returns in the form of carried interest, or if they were investments in capital interests on terms similar to those of outside investors.[74] In 2014, we found that there were challenges regarding the usefulness, reliability, and comparability of plan asset information on Form 5500s—the annual report that employee benefit plans file with DOL.[75] These challenges, identified by Form 5500 stakeholders, included a lack of detailed information on plan assets for filers with fewer than 100 participants that are not required to file a Schedule H, which is a part of Form 5500 detailing a plan's assets.[76] We recommended, among other things, that DOL and other agencies responsible for administering Form 5500 revise Schedule H to provide more transparency into plan investments.[77]

Drawing on public filings with the SEC we determined that the private equity firm and hedge funds enabling employees to invest in their own funds charge their outside investors a performance fee that amounts to a carried interest in these funds. But, despite recently expanded reporting requirements by SEC on private equity firms and hedge funds, we could not determine how general partners distribute carried interest among various partnership interests, such as those held by employees investing in employer-sponsored plans.[78] Although the private equity firm and hedge funds disclosed that they held a carried interest in their funds, they did not disclose the general partner's internal distribution of this carried interest among key employees (see appendix IV for an example of how a key employee can invest in a portion of the general partner's carried interest through a profits interest). Absent increased transparency in filings with DOL documenting the assets held in employer plans and information about how the profits of private equity firms and hedge funds are distributed among various types of partnership interests, IRS will have difficulty assessing the kinds of assets being rolled into IRAs.

Hedge Funds and a Private Equity Firm that Allow Their Employees to Invest in Their Own Funds

Hedge fund 401(k) profit sharing plan ($18 million in assets)

Employees invest more than 53 percent of plan assets in the employer's funds.

Hedge fund 401(k) ($75 million in assets)

Employees invest more than 90 percent of plan assets in the employer's funds.

Hedge fund IRA plan ($103 million in assets)

Employees may invest 100 percent of their contributions in the employer's funds.

Hedge fund 401(k) profit sharing plan ($123 million in assets)

Employees invest almost 97 percent of plan assets in the employer's funds.

Private equity fund profit sharing plan ($191 million in assets)

Employees invest almost 28 percent of plan assets in the employer's funds.

Source: GAO analysis of four hedge funds' and one private equity firm's Form 5500 filings with the Department of Labor, December 31, 2012. | GAO-15-16

Given the difficultly and uncertainty IRS faces in selecting and pursuing potential instances of noncompliance based on valuation, a few individuals can realize tax advantages from IRAs that substantially exceed those available to the vast majority of investors. According to IRS officials, any additional information about assets that have been rolled over into IRAs would be helpful. IRS officials told us that expanded information could reduce the considerable time and cost of pursuing cases of potential noncompliance based on the valuation of assets in IRAs. DOL filings for employer-sponsored plans in some instances do not contain any detail on the assets held by a plan. However, even when a description of assets is included, neither DOL nor SEC filings include information on whether the general partner distributes carried interest to profits interests held by key employees in a DC plan. This information could help IRS understand the potential investment returns that could have been expected to accrue to a profits interest rolled into an IRA and thus determine if the initial valuation of the profits interest was appropriate. Without this additional detail it will continue to be hard for IRS to determine the magnitude of investment returns a profits interest held in an IRA could reasonably be expected to generate. Such information could be used to determine how assets in IRAs might appropriately have been initially valued. Our prior work has shown that an important feature that helped DB plan sponsors successfully address the challenges of investing in private equity funds and hedge funds includes the transparent disclosure of fees such as carried interest.[79]

Congress Likely Did Not Intend IRAs to Result in Tax-Favored Accumulations of Funds beyond Those Reasonably Necessary to Support Individuals in Retirement

Congress enacted ERISA to promote opportunities for individuals to accumulate resources for their retirement and IRAs were originally authorized largely to ensure equitable tax treatment for individuals without access to an employer-sponsored plan. Congress envisioned that these individuals would be the most likely to establish and rely on IRAs. IRAs provide a way for individuals not covered by employer-sponsored plans to save for retirement and give retiring workers or individuals changing jobs a way to preserve assets from employer-sponsored DC plans by allowing them to roll over, or transfer plan assets into IRAs. Prior to this, individuals not covered by an employer-sponsored plan could not save for retirement under the favorable tax treatment afforded to participants of employer-sponsored plans. This resulted in inequitable tax treatment of individuals not covered by employer-sponsored plans. Congress cited the need, on the basis of equitable tax treatment, to create IRAs and grant these individuals a limited tax deduction on their retirement savings.[80] Similarly, the Taxpayer Relief Act of 1997 created Roth IRAs, which extended tax incentives to individuals who, based on their income, were ineligible to make tax deductible contributions to traditional IRAs. It extended retirement tax incentives to individuals who made just enough that they could not benefit from the deductibility of contributions to traditional IRAs.

Since Congress created traditional and Roth IRAs, they have become the key retirement savings vehicles for many individuals not covered by employer-sponsored plans, including small business owners and independent contractors. But a small number of individuals have found IRAs, and in particular Roth IRAs, to be an advantageous investment vehicle for purchasing disproportionately profitable assets at a low initial value, or transferring such assets from employer-sponsored plans, without paying more than a nominal amount of tax on their gains. The use of IRAs permits these individuals to accumulate far more in resources, under favorable tax treatment, than may be reasonably necessary to support them in retirement.

Through ERISA, Congress also amended the Internal Revenue Code to impose certain limits on employer-sponsored plans seeking preferential tax treatment.[81] Specifically, Congress established a limit on benefit payments from employer-sponsored DB plans and contribution limits on DC plans.[82] Congress established similar contribution limits on IRAs. Congress imposed these limits to prevent the tax-favored accumulation of balances "completely out of proportion to the reasonable needs of individuals for a dignified level of retirement income."[83]

Forty years after the enactment of ERISA, some in Congress continue to be concerned with the fairness of tax-favored retirement balances. In a 2012 letter to IRS, some members of Congress expressed concern that strategies for accumulating large IRAs by using very low valuations might be widespread among certain higher-income individuals. Members of Congress also noted the opportunity to address inequities stemming from the inappropriate use of retirement tax benefits presented by Congress's current efforts to reform the broader tax code. In a 2012 hearing on tax reform and tax-favored retirement accounts, the Chairman of the House Ways and Means Committee stressed the importance of increasing participation in retirement accounts by low- and middle-income taxpayers, and ensuring that retirement tax benefits are effectively and appropriately targeted.

We have long recommended greater scrutiny of tax expenditures, such as the deferral of taxation on retirement savings in traditional DC plans and IRAs and the ability to essentially pay taxes up front on contributions to designated Roth accounts in DC plans and to Roth IRAs, in exchange for tax-free investment earnings and distributions.[84] We developed criteria to assist policymakers in assessing tax expenditures.[85] These criteria include the following.

- Identifying the tax expenditure's purpose, a necessary first step in assessing its performance.
- Considering the fairness and equity of the tax expenditure. For example the criteria include determining who benefits from the tax expenditure, and whether taxpayers with different abilities to pay receive different benefits from the tax expenditure.[86]
- Determining the budget consequences of the tax expenditure, or, how much the tax expenditure costs the government in forgone tax revenue. Specifically, the criteria suggest policymakers consider options for limiting revenue losses from the tax expenditure, for example, by capping the aggregate amount taxpayers can claim.

In the absence of changes by Congress to current tax incentives for retirement savings, certain individuals with the resources to do so will likely continue to engage in sophisticated investment strategies that effectively change their DC plan or IRA from an account for modest retirement savings into a tax-advantaged investment vehicle for accumulating significant wealth. This will be done through investments unavailable to most taxpayers. IRS officials reported in 2012 that longterm revenue losses to the federal government from IRA abuses had increased significantly since 2004, when IRS first created an Issue Management Team (IMT) to address this issue. IRS officials warned that, without legislative change, certain IRA strategies could conceivably result in thousands of families living for generations without the need to contribute to retirement accounts or pay federal income tax. In discussions with industry stakeholders and government officials, a number of proposals have been raised to address the accumulation of large IRAs. Two approaches are restricting the types of assets that can be held in IRAs or imposing a minimum valuation requirement on assets in IRAs. For example, a minimum required purchase price of one dollar per share could prevent the founders of companies from purchasing millions of nonpublicly traded shares within IRA contribution limits. Additionally, a limit on the amount of accumulations allowed in DC plans and IRAs is another approach. Similarly, Treasury officials have proposed limiting contributions to IRAs once a certain level of savings has been achieved.

IRS Has Dedicated Resources to IRA Compliance but Faces Challenges with Nonpublicly Traded IRA Investments

IRS Relies on the Automated Underreporter Program and Field Examinations to Enforce IRA Tax Laws and Has Targeted Abusive IRA Transactions

Within the Wage and Investment (W&I) division, the Automated Underreporter Program (AUR) covers a broad range of taxpayers with IRAs and is IRS's primary means of detecting noncompliance with contribution and distribution requirements.[87] In tax year 2010 (the last full available year), AUR assessed additional taxes of $88 million for about 226,000 tax returns with IRA discrepancies.

IRS continues to take action aimed at noncompliance by taxpayers who fail to take required minimum distributions or contribute more than the allowable limits. In addition to outreach efforts targeting these rules, W&I held two tests sending taxpayers soft notices—letters that require no action on the taxpayer's part but encourage the taxpayer to check his or her return for errors. These tests were intended to improve IRA compliance without IRS having to invest audit resources.

The December 2013 test reminded taxpayers that they need to take a required distribution, and the February 2014 test targeted taxpayers who made excess contributions. As of October 2014, IRS was collecting test data, such as whether taxpayers plan to correct the errors, for use in evaluating future soft notice efforts or whether other compliance activities are needed.

IRS's Small Business/Self-Employed (SB/SE) division uses field examinations to pursue more complex tax return cases, including those that could involve the multimillion dollar IRA strategies described above. In fiscal year 2013, field examiners audited IRA issues on 1,588 returns and recommended $3.3 million in additional taxes, representing 0.3 percent of SB/SE examinations and 1.1 percent of total tax adjustments for that year. SB/SE training for new revenue agents and tax compliance officers covers specifics on enforcing IRA tax laws.

Examiner job aides, also called lead sheets, emphasize investigating all of the taxpayers' contributions over time to determine if the taxpayers are noncompliant with their reporting. IRS's Engineering Department, which is part of the Large Business and International (LB&I) division, also provides in-house expertise on valuation issues and can be called upon when IRS discovers a valuation issue during an examination. SB/SE examination officials have developed additional guidance on IRAs for examiners' continuing professional education.

SB/SE also has conducted special compliance initiative projects (CIP) to identify patterns of IRA noncompliance and better allocate examination resources and education efforts. Since 2007, CIPs have targeted excess contributions, early distributions, and taxes owed on Roth IRA conversions.

Also led by SB/SE examiners, the Abusive Transactions and Technical Issues (ATTI) Program has targeted abusive schemes using IRAs. ATTI generally gets leads for investigating individuals involved in IRA schemes from investigations and monitoring of promoters who market tax shelters. In 2012 (the last full year of available data), ATTI examined 95 taxpayers and assessed additional taxes totaling $15 million in IRA-related cases. Two types of abusive IRA transactions that IRS examination officials said they have focused on include:

- **Roth IRA "stuffing":** This scheme involves shifting value through transactions that disguise Roth IRA contributions exceeding annual IRA limits, such as selling receivables at less than fair market value to a Roth IRA.
  In 2004, IRS determined that this abusive tax avoidance shelter is a listed transaction that taxpayers must report to IRS.[88] Because IRA stuffing can involve improper valuation, IRS's efforts in this area have the potential to detect abuse in asset valuation in the strategies that stakeholders told us could lead to multimillion dollar IRAs. In a 2012 briefing document, IRS examination officials said that noncompliance using this approach "could conceivably result in thousands of families living for generations without the need to contribute or pay federal income tax. IRS continues to monitor taxpayer attempts at Roth IRA stuffing.
- **Self-dealing within an IRA:** These are prohibited transactions in which a taxpayer in control of the IRA's asset management ultimately benefits from the asset before retirement in violation of tax laws.[89] Examples are having the IRA purchase a beachfront home as a rental, but the taxpayer uses it for herself, or an IRA owner drawing a salary from an IRA-invested business.

Other IRS enforcement programs do not target IRA noncompliance but may refer IRA-related cases for field examination. Within LB&I, the Global High Wealth industry unit targets individual taxpayers with assets or earnings of tens of millions of dollars and, in looking at their complete financial picture and the enterprises they control, may notice possible noncompliance with a taxpayer's IRA.

Similarly, IRS Estate and Gift tax examiners may detect possible IRA noncompliance in reviewing a decedent's estate tax return. IRS enforcement officials from SB/SE and TE/GE said that reliance on referrals from one division to another requires coordination, without which IRS may be vulnerable to noncompliance that spans division expertise. For example, asset valuation issues may originate in an employer DC plan before being rolled over to an IRA.

TE/GE examiners would be responsible for valuation issues within a DC plan, and it may be many years before the noncompliance is discovered by an examiner auditing an individual tax return.

In 2008, IRS chartered an IMT—including representatives from SB/SE and TE/GE—to develop IRS-wide strategies and solutions to curb the proliferation of IRA abuse and potentially clarify and strengthen IRA tax laws.

In 2009, the IMT suggested collecting additional data from custodians holding IRAs with hard-to-value nonpublic assets as an immediate step supporting a longer term strategy recommending legislative changes, among other things, to limit the types of IRA investments. By 2012, without progress on having IRS's legislative proposals considered by Treasury, the IMT developed an interim strategy for IRS to move forward with increased data collection and draw more attention to IRA noncompliance.

IRS Plans to Collect Data to Identify IRAs with Riskier Nonpublic Assets, and Examiner Use Depends on Digitizing the Data

IRS plans to evaluate more data on hard-to-value IRA assets that would help to refine its enforcement efforts. For tax year 2014 (to be filed in 2015), IRS Form 5498 has new boxes for custodians to report the portion of the IRA FMV attributable to nonmarket assets as well as a box with codes describing the type of nonmarket assets, as shown in figure 9. Also for tax year 2014, custodians are to report similar information on Form 1099-R identifying distributions of IRA assets that do not have a readily available FMV. The new reporting is optional for 2014, and IRS plans to require custodians to provide the information for tax year 2015 (to be filed in 2016). As of September 2014, IRS officials said that they will continue to assess comments from stakeholders about the form changes, but IRS does not anticipate changes to the timeline.

SB/SE examination officials said that the new Form 5498 data will help them better identify taxpayers with IRAs invested in nonpublicly traded assets. They said the data also will help them review the history of FMV reported.

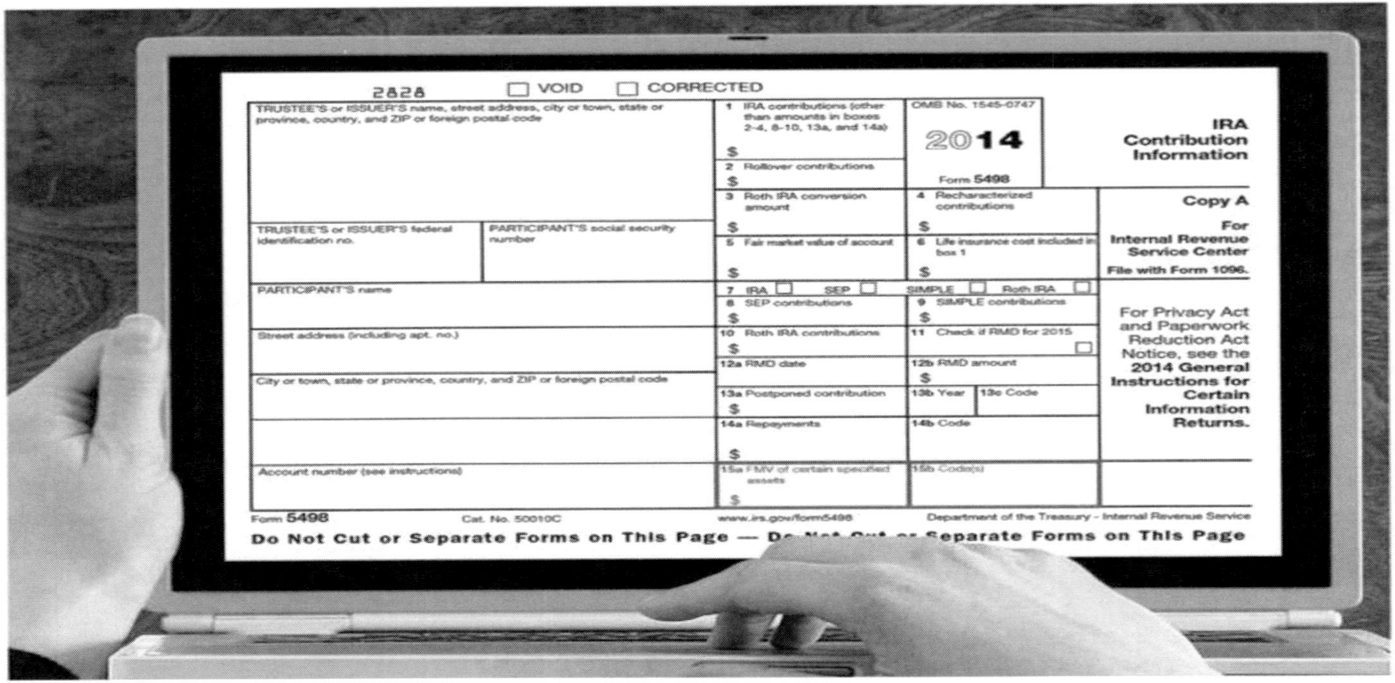

Source: GAO summary of IRS information; PhotoDisc and IRS (images). | GAO-15-16.

Figure 9. Types of Assets Individual Retirement Account Custodians Will Identify on Form 5498 Starting in Tax Year 2014.

(See Appendix V for an expanded version of Figure 9).

Efficient use of the new Form 5498 and 1099-R data for examination case selection hinges on IRS's ability to compile and analyze the new information on nonpublicly traded assets types and FMV. Custodians, like other third-party reporters, must file electronically if they submit 250 or more of one kind of information return.[90] A specialty custodian submitting fewer than 250 forms currently may file on paper. An IRS Submissions Processing official told us about 1,400 custodians submitted only paper forms in tax year 2012. As previously reported, IRS historically has limited the use of electronically filed data for classification to only the types of data that are transcribed from paper-filed returns to assure that paper-filed returns are treated the same as electronic returns[91] Unless the new information is available electronically—most commonly achieved through data transcription—IRS classifiers will not be able to fully use the new information, undercutting IRS's intention to more systematically identify IRAs with greater risk of noncompliance.

W&I's Submission Processing office has requested transcription of the new IRA asset-type reporting that will be mandatory for 2015 forms to be filed in 2016. IRS prioritizes transcribing data based on a number of factors, such as physical capacity, as well as resources and funding. In June 2014, we reported that IRS faces budget uncertainty and indications are that its funding will be constrained for the foreseeable future.[92] As of October 2014, IRS has not finalized plans for making the data available electronically. The cost of transcribing the new data would be relatively small, as IRS estimated that about 9,000 Form 5498 submissions were filed on paper in 2013 out of more than 118 million filings.[93] A similarly small percentage of Form 1099-R filings go to IRS on paper. IRS estimated for us that the annual labor cost for transcribing the forms would be $2,322 to $12,210.[94] However, noncompliance with IRA rules can result in sizable revenue losses if IRA transactions are misreported continuously over many years.

Custodian and taxpayer behavior could change because of heightened attention on nonpublic IRA assets with the new reporting and the potential for greater IRS scrutiny. Some custodians already restrict IRAs to holding only publicly traded investments, and the additional reporting for alternative assets may dissuade other custodians from holding IRAs with such assets. Furthermore, taxpayers who want to manipulate valuations will have less room to do so, since custodians will still report on the type of asset in the account. Increased reporting on alternative assets by custodians to IRS may encourage better compliance by some taxpayers. According to IRS examination and Chief Counsel officials, however, custodians may not always be able to get accurate asset information about IRAs if the IRA owner has day-to-day investment control, which could lead to unreliable Form 5498 reporting of asset types and FMV. It may be difficult to apply general penalties to custodians for third-party misreporting if the IRA owner is the source of the inaccurate FMV data.

IRS Has Tried to Address Challenges in Auditing the Valuation of Nonpublic IRA Assets and Detecting Prohibited Transactions

SB/SE examination officials said IRA noncompliance is difficult to pursue for a variety of reasons. First, some IRA cases—including the large-dollar IRA accumulation strategies cited by financial industry stakeholders—are about valuation issues. IRS officials said these issues are expensive to audit and often must be pursued through litigation in court. For example, IRS examination officials said that determining that an asset was undervalued cannot be made without expensive auditing and litigation. Each case requires extensive resources, including significant time of examiners, engineers, appraisers, appeals officers, and attorneys and fees to obtain appraisals from external contractors, according to examination officials. Examination and Chief Counsel officials said that valuation cases are a matter of opinion, and typically involve taxpayers with lots of resources. Taxpayers can find appraisers who will value assets in an IRA the way they want, and IRS faces difficulty in that it has to procure and present its expert testimony about the valuation. An improper valuation made many years prior to its discovery by SB/SE also may fall outside the 3-year examination statute of limitations discussed above.[95]

Another challenge is uncertainty about how DOL and the courts might rule on a particular set of facts in potential prohibited transaction cases or the exemptions to prohibited transaction rules that DOL might grant. IRS examination and Chief Counsel officials said that in their informal consultation process, they have a good working relationship with DOL, and DOL officials generally agreed with this characterization. However, IRS Chief Counsel officials said "things can get complicated" between DOL setting the rules and IRS enforcing them during audits, as IRS may not be sure whether DOL thinks a particular transaction is legitimate.[96] DOL also may grant exemptions to employer-sponsored IRA plans that IRS otherwise could have deemed noncompliant. When possible prohibited transactions arise during examination that might require DOL input, IRS examination officials reach out to DOL through TE/GE to ensure that IRS understands the ruling on the transaction correctly.[97] As with valuation, the statute of limitations poses obstacles to pursing prohibited transactions. According to IRS, abuses frequently are not reflected on any filed tax return and are difficult to detect within the general 3-year statute of limitation period. When certain prohibited transactions occur, the IRA loses its tax-favored status and is treated as distributing all of its assets at the FMV on the first day of the year when the prohibited transaction occurred. Once IRS examiners detect a prohibited transaction, the taxpayer can dispute when the income should have been reported.

There are few judicial opinions regarding prohibited transactions, according to IRS officials. They also said that the 2013 Tax Court ruling in *Peek v. Commissioner* (see text box) sets a useful precedent for increased IRS enforcement of the prohibited transaction in more complex, higher dollar value cases.[98] Building on *Peek*, SB/SE is working on honing procedures for examiners to use in determining whether an IRA case may have violated prohibited transactions that are similar to the *Peek* case. IRS examination officials said that the process would help IRS make decisions about the validity of transactions without having to go to DOL for every case. They said that *Peek* will help them more confidently identify prohibited transactions and encourage custodians as well as IRA owners and their advisors to be more aware of what is noncompliant. As of September 2014, IRS said the fact-pattern was an ongoing effort.

Peek v. Commissioner Summary

Two individuals, Lawrence Peek and Darrell Fleck, each established traditional IRAs, rolled over funds from existing retirement accounts, set up a new corporation, and sold all of the stock of the corporation to the IRAs. They then used the funds from the sale of the stock to buy the assets of a business and executed personal loan guaranties with respect to that purchase. Thereafter, Peek and Fleck converted their traditional IRAs into Roth IRAs funded by the same stock. The Roth IRAs subsequently sold the now-significantly appreciated stock of the corporation and treated the gain as deferred. IRS asserted deficiencies against Peek and Fleck on the grounds that the loan guaranties were prohibited transactions. The Tax Court agreed and held that Internal Revenue Code § 4975(c)(1)(B) prohibits taxpayers from making loan guaranties either directly to their IRAs or indirectly to their IRAs through an entity owned by the IRAs.

The Court further held that the IRAs ceased to qualify as IRAs when the prohibited transactions originally occurred and therefore the Roth IRAs were also void because the prohibited transaction continued as to those accounts. The Court also upheld accuracy-related penalties imposed by IRS.

Peek and Fleck appealed the Tax Court decision. As of October, 10, 2014, the case before the Tenth Circuit Court of Appeals was still pending.

Source: Peek v. Commission 140 T.C. 216 (2013). | GAO-15-16.

In 2009, the IMT proposed several legislative changes to address enforcement challenges IRS encounters in auditing IRA activity. These include: (1) limiting the types of investments IRAs can make to publicly traded or otherwise marketable securities with a readily ascertainable fair market value; (2) expanding the definition under "disqualified person" to address work performed by the IRA beneficiary's siblings on behalf of the IRA-owned entity or operation; and (3) expanding the statute of limitations in Internal Revenue Code Sec. 6501 to 6 years for all IRA activity.[99] The team's 2009 legislative recommendations were approved by the Service-wide Compliance Strategy Executive Steering Committee in 2010.[100] In 2012, the issue management team met again to study abusive IRA trends and continued to recommend legislative change. As of September 2014, no further action has taken place. Ultimately, Treasury has to review all tax legislative proposals and presents the administration's tax proposals for congressional consideration. In the fiscal year 2014 and 2015 budgets, Treasury proposed an overall cap on tax-favored retirement saving accumulations.[101]

As IRS begins collecting data on nonpublic IRA assets from Form 5498, it will be positioned to quantify the number of IRAs and associated FMV held in hard-to-value asset types with greater compliance risk. As discussed above, the new asset-type data—if available electronically— will help IRS in selecting examination cases. IRS examination officials said that research using the new data could aid in developing the business case for further action to address noncompliance. Specifically, additional research by IRS could help to evaluate the feasibility of the proposals to require greater disclosure of potentially undervalued asset types as transactions of interest or require reporting of prohibited transactions as listed transactions. Moving forward with a service-wide strategy to target enforcement efforts would hinge on IRS first conducting the research to understand how many taxpayers and the reported amounts of IRA assets are at risk of noncompliance.

IRS Outreach and Education Increase Taxpayer Understanding of Complex IRA Rules but Are Not Explicit about the Risk of Alternative Investment Noncompliance

IRS has included taxpayer service and outreach in its strategies to improve compliance with IRA tax laws. As we reported in 2008, financial industry organizations and advisor representatives we interviewed complimented IRS *Publication 590 Individual Retirement Arrangements (IRAs)* (*Publication 590*) for translating the many complicated IRA contribution and distributions rules into "plain English" to help taxpayers comply.[102] IRS continues to target outreach to help taxpayers understand minimum distribution requirements and IRA contribution limits.

Insights about noncompliance detected by enforcement can help IRS identify opportunities to educate taxpayers on how to better comply. IRS has a system for examiners to communicate issues to IRS's external communication office, Communication and Stakeholder Outreach. ATTI chairs an emerging issues team that meets quarterly to address new compliance risks and may identify issues for the communications office. Research identifying the numbers and types of custodians and taxpayers holding hard-to-value assets could also help IRS target outreach activities and strategies for improving compliance with IRA asset valuation and prohibited transaction requirements. For example, IRS could provide notices targeting custodians and taxpayers with nonpublic IRA assets with a reminder about their responsibilities and the potential tax consequences of engaging in self-dealing and other prohibited transactions.

Examination officials said one challenge in educating the public is a promoter industry that advertises IRAs with alternative assets that also give taxpayers "checkbook access" (i.e., more control over IRA investment choices compared to other IRAs). These promoters might not disclose the compliance risks and responsibilities taxpayers take on when investing in nonpublicly traded assets. The promoters' advertising may leave less sophisticated taxpayers at risk for unintentional noncompliance with IRA laws. IRS guidance targeting attention on the compliance responsibilities and risks inherent in investing in nonpublic IRA assets and directly controlling IRA assets could help taxpayers make more informed decisions. In 2009, IRS issued a revised publication explicitly warning that it does not approve or endorse particular types of assets for IRAs.[103] Targeted at protecting taxpayers from fraudulent IRA sales pitches, this notice advises taxpayers to proceed with caution when encouraged to invest in a general partnership or limited liability company. *Publication 590* describes what prohibited transactions are but does not make the explicit connection that certain asset types pose greater potential for prohibited transactions. As a result, some taxpayers may be unaware that certain IRA investment decisions have greater risks for committing prohibited transactions that could trigger loss of their IRAs' tax-favored status. In contrast, for custodians, the IRS instructions for Forms 5498 and 1099-R plainly state that nonpublic assets and assets under IRA owner control have a greater potential for prohibited transactions. General reminders are a low cost way to draw attention and caution taxpayers about the compliance risks associated with certain IRA choices.

CONCLUSION

Congress envisioned IRAs as a moderate tax benefit to help individuals not covered by employer-sponsored plans to obtain income sufficient for a secure retirement, not as a vehicle for accumulating significant tax-preferred wealth. Without further consideration from Congress, individuals with these limited, occupationally related opportunities to engage in sophisticated investment strategies may accumulate considerable tax-preferred wealth in IRAs. The result is a revenue loss to the federal government through a circumvention of the longstanding rationale for IRA contribution limits. However, Congress can reorient existing laws to address the excesses of these strategies, so that all taxpayers have similar opportunities to reap the benefits of IRAs. Congress could, for example, address the build-up of unnecessarily large IRAs in a variety of ways: by limiting the types of investments held in IRAs, enforcing standards such as a minimum required value for investments in an IRA, or by setting a ceiling on accumulations in an IRA and requiring an immediate distribution of balances above that ceiling. Without such a readjustment, the intended broad-based tax benefits of IRAs will continue to be skewed towards a select group of investors.

With respect to individual taxes, IRS has dedicated enforcement resources to identifying taxpayers who may be building IRA balances improperly. It is critical to collect data on alternative IRA assets with a higher risk of noncompliance, given that the valuation issues at the heart of the strategies to build large IRAs pose high costs for IRS enforcement and carry a risk of IRS failing to prove wrongdoing in court. Moving forward, IRS has the opportunity to use the data to further research IRA noncompliance, such as whether IRAs invested in nonpublicly traded shares are predicated on noncompliance, as industry stakeholders we spoke with allege. Such research is a necessary step toward designating strategies leading to high-dollar IRAs as problematic and targeting examination resources efficiently. Positioning IRS to take full advantage of the new Form 5498 data hinges on IRS digitizing the data for compliance case selection and examination. While IRS estimates capturing the data for the relatively few paper filing would add small costs to processing the forms, the benefits—in terms of less forgone revenue, a greater perception of a fair tax system, and better use of enforcement resources—would outweigh those costs.

Existing data from DOL and SEC on employer-sponsored plans and the performance fees charged by private equity firms and hedge funds provide information that could also assist IRS in assessing the valuation of assets in IRAs. We previously recommended that DOL and others improve the usefulness, reliability, and comparability of Form 5500 data in part by providing more transparency into assets held in employer-sponsored plans. Providing this information is important because it helps regulators better understand the types of assets held in tax-favored retirement accounts. If DOL were required to improve the transparency of assets held in employer-sponsored plans, IRS could have better information on where the assets in a large IRA may have originated. In addition, data about how private equity firms and hedge funds distribute their carried interest could also be of use to IRS as it decides whether to move forward with a case against an IRA owner based on valuation.

The new asset-type data also gives IRS more information about IRAs at greater risk for self-dealing abuse and other prohibited transactions. As IRS increases it examination presence, evidence on the obstacles encountered in pursuing prohibited transactions and noncompliant activity engaged in for years may demonstrate whether it would be worthwhile to change the current 3-year statute of limitations for tax assessment with regard to IRAs.

In an environment where less-sophisticated taxpayers can be lured by "checkbook access" to IRAs invested in unconventional assets, IRS has an opportunity to warn taxpayers about the added responsibilities and compliance risks inherent in investing and managing alternative assets in IRAs. Current IRA guidance aimed at taxpayers does not acknowledge the greater risks for committing prohibited transactions—even though Form 5498 instructions for custodians plainly make this point. Without an explicit caution, taxpayers may continue to make un-informed decisions about IRA investments that put them at a greater risk of noncompliance and loss of their IRAs' tax-favored status.

MATTER FOR CONGRESSIONAL CONSIDERATION

To promote retirement savings without creating permanent tax-favored accounts for a small segment of the population, Congress should consider revisiting the use of IRAs to accumulate large balances and consider ways to improve the equity of the existing tax expenditure on IRAs. Options could include limits on (1) the types of assets permitted in IRAs, (2) the minimum valuation for an asset purchased by an IRA, or (3) the amount of assets that can be accumulated in IRAs and employer-sponsored plans that get preferential tax treatment.

RECOMMENDATIONS FOR EXECUTIVE ACTION

We are making five recommendations to the Commissioner of Internal Revenue.

To improve IRS's ability to detect and pursue noncompliance associated with undervalued assets sheltered in IRAs and prohibited transactions, we recommend that the Commissioner of Internal Revenue:

- Approve plans to fully compile and digitize the new data from electronic and paper-filed Form 5498s to ensure the efficient use of the information on nonpublicly traded IRA assets.
- Conduct research using the new Form 5498 data to identify IRAs holding nonpublic asset types, such as profits interests in private equity firms and hedge funds, and use that information for an IRS-wide strategy to target enforcement efforts.
- Work in consultation with the Department of the Treasury on a legislative proposal to expand the statute of limitations on IRA noncompliance to help IRS pursue valuation-related misreporting and prohibited transactions that may have originated outside the current statute's 3-year window.

To help taxpayers better understand compliance risks associated with certain IRA choices and improve compliance, we recommend that the Commissioner of Revenue:

- Building on research data on IRAs holding nonpublic assets, identify options to provide outreach targeting taxpayers with nonpublic IRA assets and their custodians, such as reminder notices that engaging in prohibited transactions can result in loss of the IRA's tax-favored status.
- Add an explicit caution in *Publication 590 Individual Retirement Arrangements (IRAs)* for taxpayers about the potential risk of committing a prohibited transaction when investing in nonpublicly traded assets or directly controlling IRA assets.

AGENCY COMMENTS

We provided a draft of this report to the Secretary of the Treasury, the Commissioner of Internal Revenue, the Secretary of Labor, and the Chair of the SEC for comment. In a September 18, 2014, letter the IRS Deputy Commissioner for Services and Enforcement generally agreed with our recommendations. On October 2, 2014, the Associate Director and Chief Counsel for SEC's Division of Investment Management voiced various legal and other concerns regarding implementation of a recommendation, designed to assist the IRS for tax reporting purposes, to expand reporting requirements on private equity firms and hedge funds to require disclosure of a general partner's agreements for distributing carried interest. As a result, we redirected the recommendation to IRS as part of an existing recommendation that IRS conduct research using new Form 5498 data on non-public IRA assets. We shared the revised recommendation with IRS officials, who continued to agree with it. IRS, Treasury, SEC, and the Department of Labor provided separate technical comments, which we incorporated in our report where appropriate.

In the IRS letter, the Deputy Commissioner emphasized that rules governing IRAs can be complicated for both the IRS and taxpayers. The Deputy Commissioner also highlighted efforts that IRS has undertaken to conduct enforcement, such as the AUR program and compliance initiative projects. The Deputy Commissioner acknowledged that IRA noncompliance can span IRS units and that the issue management team allowed cross-functional coordination to address noncompliance.

IRS agreed with our assessment that digitizing IRA information return data could improve case selection. However, the Deputy Commissioner said that IRS is faced with competing funding priorities and will continue to evaluate the priority of digitizing additional Form 5498 information.

IRS also agreed to conduct research using the new Form 5498 data to identify IRAs holding nonpublic assets and use the information for an IRS-wide strategy to target enforcement efforts. The Deputy Commissioner said that the SB/SE Abusive Transactions and Technical Issues function has begun to develop research objectives to refine enforcement efforts using the additional information that IRS will obtain from the revised Form 5498 data.

The Deputy Commissioner agreed that legislation to extend the period of limitations for assessment of tax associated with IRA noncompliance would remove an obstacle to IRS efforts to pursue identified IRA noncompliance. The Deputy Commissioner added that IRS will discuss with Treasury proposals regarding the statute of limitations on assessing tax associated with IRA noncompliance.

The Deputy Commissioner said IRS agreed to build on research data on IRAs holding nonpublic assets to identify options to provide outreach, such as reminder notices. The Deputy Commissioner said that as IRS analyzes the data, it will identify options to provide targeted outreach to taxpayers with IRAs holding such assets to increase awareness of prohibited transaction rules and penalties for failure to comply with these rules.

The Deputy Commissioner agreed with our recommendation to add an explicit caution in *Publication 590* for taxpayers about the risk of committing a prohibited transaction when investing in nonpublicly traded assets or directly controlling IRA assets.

Sincerely yours,
James R. McTigue, Jr. Director,
Tax Issues Strategic Issues

Charles A. Jeszeck
Director,
Education, Workforce, and Income Security

APPENDIX I: OBJECTIVES, SCOPE, AND METHODOLOGY

This report: (1) describes the number and types of taxpayers with individual retirement accounts (IRA) and the size of IRA balances in terms of aggregate fair market value (FMV), adjusted gross income (AGI), filing status and age; (2) examines how IRA balances can become large; and (3) assesses how the Internal Revenue Service (IRS) ensures that taxpayers with IRAs comply with IRA tax laws.

Measuring IRA Balances and What Is Considered Large

To describe the taxpayers with IRAs by the accumulated balances in terms of FMV, AGI, filing status and age, we used an Internal Revenue Service (IRS) Statistics of Income (SOI) sample of individual income tax returns for tax year 2011 (the most recent year available) as well as IRS "IRA Contribution Information" Form 5498 data associated with the SOI sample. Our analysis of SOI statistical data is subject to sampling errors because the SOI data are based on a sample of tax returns as filed.[1] In addition, the data do not reflect IRS audit results. The SOI sample of individual income tax returns does not include those who do not file a return. However, some IRA custodians submitted Form 5498s on nonfilers. An IRS official said SOI attempts to include additional information on nonfilers by sampling documents, including Form 5498s, which have no associated individual income tax returns. Form 5498 filings without a matching return were sampled at approximately 1:1,000. In 2011, about 3,800 nonfilers were sampled, none of whom had unusually large IRA balances.

We aggregated the total FMV for all IRAs associated with a return (including inherited IRAs as IRS data do not readily identify inherited IRAs) to obtain an accumulated IRA balance. We used the taxpayers as our unit of analysis. Taxpayers filing joint returns are treated as a single unit and the IRAs owned by both spouses are aggregated. Our analysis of SOI data is subject to errors from sampling as well as from the small sample of returns with higher IRA balances. About 99 percent of taxpayers with IRAs have accumulated balances of $1 million or less. However our group of interest was that small group of taxpayers with large IRA balances and estimates based on this small group may not be precise and have very wide associated confidence intervals. Because of the skewness of the distribution for taxpayers with IRA balances greater than $25 million, we used a statistical technique referred to as bootstrapping or resampling to estimate the confidence interval.

About 5 percent of the estimated taxpayers with IRAs had at least one associated IRA with blank FMV information. We treated the blank FMVs as zeros. If these IRAs did not, in fact, have zero balances, they could affect our estimates' upper bound considerably. However, IRS officials told us they generally treat blank FMVs as zeros based on their understanding of IRA custodians filing practice. We compared Form 5498 information for particular IRA owners to information from their income tax and Form 1099R information returns. Working with IRS, we identified a number of reasons why blank FMVs could be zeros such as: (1) the entire account balance was distributed; (2) the balance was rolled over to another IRA; (3) the owner of the IRA was deceased and IRA assets were transferred to a beneficiary; (4) tax year contributions were made to a new IRA account for a prior calendar year.

In addition to the number of taxpayers and FMVs for their aggregated IRAs, we presented the data for two separate groups: 1) those with IRA balances of $1 million or less and 2) those with IRA balances of more than $5 million and the confidence intervals associated with the estimates. We do not report on taxpayers with IRA balances greater than $1 million to $5 million to avoid disclosure of taxpayer information.

We compared the two groups on three types of IRAs—traditional, Roth, and other IRAs that included employer-sponsored SEP and SIMPLE IRAs. We used eight categories of AGI, which is the individual's gross income minus adjustments that include deductions for trade or business expenses, losses from the sale or exchange of property, contributions to pension and other retirement plans and alimony payments. Our AGI categories were

- $0 or less,
- $1 to $20,000,
- $20,001 to $50,000,
- $50,001 to $100,000,
- $100,001 to $200,000,
- $200,001 to $500,000,
- $500,001 to $1,000,000, and
- Greater than $1,000,000.

About 1 percent to 2 percent of the taxpayers reported zero AGI. We did not use the modified AGI used to determine eligibility for IRA contributions which added certain items such as foreign housing expenses and student loan deductions back to the AGI. For the filing status comparison, we used three categories—single, married filing jointly and others, which included married filers who were filing separately, head of household, and qualifying widow(er). For the comparison of age we used 2 categories: those younger than age 65 and those age 65 and older. As our unit of analysis was the taxpaying unit, our age-65-and-older category included the filer, spouse, or both who were age 65 or older. To assess the reliability of the data we used, we reviewed IRS documentation and interviewed agency officials familiar with the data. We determined that these data were sufficiently reliable for the purposes of this report. However, the IRS SOI sample may not provide a precise estimate of the number of taxpayers or other quantities when the number of taxpayers in a particular reporting group is very small.[2]

To provide perspective on what might be considered a large IRA, we illustrated how much an individual could potentially accumulate in an IRA based on the statutory limits on annual contributions (see table 5) Specifically, we developed one scenario assuming maximum IRA contributions from 1975 through 2011 (the same year as our SOI analysis). Given that rollovers from employer plans have become the predominant source of funds into IRAs, we also developed a second scenario assuming the maximum combined employer and employee contributions from 1980 to 2011. [3] For simplicity, the defined contribution (DC) plan scenario assumed an individual participating in a single employer plan and rolling over a DC balance into a newly established IRA in 2011.[4] Both scenarios also assumed maximum catch-up contribution for individuals age 50 and older beginning in 2002. Table 6 shows the assumed contributions for the IRA and DC plan scenarios. The two scenarios are intended to illustrate the upper bound on total contributions over time based on the statutory annual limits for each type of tax-preferred retirement account and do not reflect how much individuals typically choose to contribute.[5] Our scenarios illustrate balances accumulated by an individual in an IRA or DC plan. For a married couple filing jointly, both spouses in concept could contribute at the statutory maximum.[6]

Table 5. Annual Contribution Dollar Limits for Individual Retirement Plans (IRA) and Defined Contribution (DC) Plans, 1975- 2014

	IRA[a]		DC plan [b]		
Year	Annual contributions	Catch-up[c]	Employee elective deferral[d]	Combined employee and employer contributions	Catch-up [c, d]
1975	1,500	N/A	N/A	N/A	N/A
1976	1,500	N/A	N/A	N/A	N/A
1977	1,500	N/A	N/A	N/A	N/A
1978	1,500	N/A	N/A	N/A	N/A
1979	1,500	N/A	N/A	N/A	N/A
1980	1,500	N/A	N/A	36,875	N/A
1981	1,500	N/A	N/A	41,500	N/A

Table 5. (Continued)

Year	IRA[a]		DC plan [b]		
	Annual contributions	Catch-up[c]	Employee elective deferral[d]	Combined employee and employer contributions	Catch-up [c, d]
1982	2,000	N/A	N/A	45,475	N/A
1983	2,000	N/A	N/A	30,000	N/A
1984	2,000	N/A	N/A	30,000	N/A
1985	2,000	N/A	N/A	30,000	N/A
1986	2,000	N/A	N/A	30,000	N/A
1987	2,000	N/A	7,000	30,000	N/A
1988	2,000	N/A	7,313	30,000	N/A
1989	2,000	N/A	7,627	30,000	N/A
1990	2,000	N/A	7,979	30,000	N/A
1991	2,000	N/A	8,475	30,000	N/A
1992	2,000	N/A	8,728	30,000	N/A
1993	2,000	N/A	8,994	30,000	N/A
1994	2,000	N/A	9,240	30,000	N/A
1995	2,000	N/A	9,240	30,000	N/A
1996	2,000	N/A	9,500	30,000	N/A
1997	2,000	N/A	9,500	30,000	N/A
1998	2,000	N/A	10,000	30,000	N/A
1999	2,000	N/A	10,000	30,000	N/A
2000	2,000	N/A	10,500	30,000	N/A
2001	2,000	N/A	10,500	35,000	N/A
2002	3,000	500	11,000	40,000	1,000
2003	3,000	500	12,000	40,000	2,000
2004	3,000	500	13,000	41,000	3,000
2005	4,000	500	14,000	42,000	4,000
2006	4,000	1,000	15,000	44,000	5,000
2007	4,000	1,000	15,500	45,000	5,000
2008	5,000	1,000	15,500	46,000	5,000
2009	5,000	1,000	16,500	49,000	5,500
2010	5,000	1,000	16,500	49,000	5,500
2011	5,000	1,000	16,500	49,000	5,500
2012	5,000	1,000	17,000	50,000	5,500
2013	5,500	1,000	17,500	51,000	5,500
2014	5,500	1,000	17,500	52,000	5,500

Source: GAO analysis of legislation and Internal Revenue Service publications.| GAO-15-16.

Notes: Generally, individual contributions to an IRA or DC plan are limited to the lesser of a specific dollar amount or 100 percent of taxable compensation for the year. For a married couple filing a joint tax return, combined IRA contributions cannot exceed the taxable compensation reported on the joint return regardless of which spouse earned the compensation. Compensation generally includes wages, salaries, professional fees, bonuses, and other amounts taxpayers receive for providing personal services and from commissions, self-employment income, alimony and separate maintenance payments taxpayers receive, and nontaxable combat pay. Taxable compensation does not include earnings and profits from property, pension or annuity income, deferred compensation received, income from partnerships for which the taxpayer did not provide services that are material income-producing factors, and any amounts excluded from income, such as foreign earned income and housing costs. N/A = Not applicable.

[a]Under the Employee Retirement Income Security Act of 1974, the contribution limit was originally the lesser of $1,500 or 15 percent of the individual's compensation for individuals not covered by employer plans. Pub. L. No. 93-406, § 2002(a), 88 Stat. 829, 958(Sept. 2, 1974). The Economic Recovery Tax Act of 1981 increased the contribution limit to the lesser of $2,000 or 100 percent of the individual's compensation and allowed contributions by those covered by employer plans. Pub. L. No. 97-34, § 311, 95 Stat. 172, 274-283 (Aug. 13, 1981). The Tax Reform Act of 1986 restricted eligibility for tax-deductible contributions for individuals covered by employer plans depending on income and filing status. Pub. L. No. 99-514, § 1101(a), 100 Stat. 2085, 2411-13 (Oct. 22, 1986). The Taxpayer Relief Act of 1997 established and allowed after-tax contributions to Roth IRAs. Pub. L. No. 105-34, § 302(a), 111 Stat. 788, 825-28 (Aug. 5, 1997). The Economic Growth and Tax Relief Reconciliation Act of 2001 increased the contribution limit in years beginning in 2002 and indexed the limit for inflation (in $500 increments) beginning in 2008 through years beginning in 2010. Pub. L. No. 107-16, §§ 601(a) and 901, 115 Stat. 38, 94-95 and 150 (June 7, 2001). The Pension Protection Act of 2006 made indexing for contribution limits permanent. Pub. L. No. 109-280, § 811, 120 Stat. 780, 996 (Aug. 17, 2006).

[b]Provisions establishing the most predominant type of DC plan, the 401(k) plan, became effective pursuant to the Revenue Act of 1978. Pub. L. No. 95-600, § 135, 92 Stat. 2763, 2785-87 (Nov. 6, 1978). The Tax Equity and Fiscal Responsibility Act of 1982 reduced the maximum allowable annual contribution to a DC plan to the lesser of $30,000 or 25 percent of compensation and suspended all cost of living adjustments until 1986. Pub. L. No. 97-324, § 235(a), 96 Stat. 324, 505 (Sept. 3, 1982). The Tax Reform Act of 1986 imposed a limit on employee elective tax-deferred contributions, but maintained the overall annual contribution limit of $30,000 for all employer and employee contributions. Pub. L. No. 99-514, § 1105(a), 100 Stat. 2085, 2417-19 (Oct. 22, 1986). The Economic Growth and Tax Relief Reconciliation Act of 2001 increased the contribution limit and the employees elective deferral for years beginning in 2002 and indexed the limit for

elective deferrals for inflation (in $500 increments) beginning in 2007 through 2010. Pub. L. No. 107-16, §§ 611(b,) (d), and 901, 115 Stat. 38, 97-98 and 150 (June 7, 2001). The Pension Protection Act of 2006 made indexing for contribution limits permanent. Pub. L. No.109-280, § 811, 120 Stat. 780, 996 (Aug. 17, 2006).

[c]Catch-up contributions for individuals age 50 and older were first allowed in 2002 pursuant to the Economic Growth and Tax Relief Reconciliation Act of 2001. Pub. L. No. 107-16, §§ 601(a) and 631(a), 115 Stat. 38, 94, 111-12 (June 7, 2001). Catch-up provisions were made permanent pursuant to the Pension Protection Act of 2006. Pub. L. No. 109-280, § 811, 120 Stat. 780, 996 (Aug. 17, 2006).

[d]The statutory elective deferral and catch-up contribution limits apply to employees who participate in 401(k), 403(b), most 457 plans, and the Thrift Savings Plan for federal employees. In addition to the statutory limits, employers may set plan-specific limits, in part, to ensure that the plans they sponsor pass statutory and regulatory requirements, such as the requirement that contributions or benefits not be skewed too heavily in favor of highly compensated employees.

Table 6. Assumed Contributions (Including Catch-up) from 1975 to 2011 under Two Illustrative Scenarios

Year	IRA maximum contributions, 1975-2011[a]	Maximum DC employer and employee contributions, 1980-2011[b]
1975	1,500	N/A
1976	1,500	N/A
1977	1,500	N/A
1978	1,500	N/A
1979	1,500	N/A
1980	1,500	36,875
1981	1,500	41,500
1982	2,000	45,475
1983	2,000	30,000
1984	2,000	30,000
1985	2,000	30,000
1986	2,000	30,000
1987	2,000	30,000
1988	2,000	30,000
1989	2,000	30,000
1990	2,000	30,000
1991	2,000	30,000
1992	2,000	30,000
1993	2,000	30,000
1994	2,000	30,000
1995	2,000	30,000

Year	IRA maximum contributions, 1975-2011a	Maximum DC employer and employee contributions, 1980-2011b
1996	2,000	30,000
1997	2,000	30,000
1998	2,000	30,000
1999	2,000	30,000
2000	2,000	30,000
2001	2,000	35,000
2002	3,500	41,000
2003	3,500	42,000
2004	3,500	44,000
2005	4,500	46,000
2006	5,000	49,000
2007	5,000	50,000
2008	6,000	51,000
2009	6,000	54,500
2010	6,000	54,500
2011	6,000	54,500
Total contributions	$99,500	$1,185,350

Source: GAO analysis | GAO-15-16.

Notes: Totals reflect maximum contributions under each scenario and do not reflect any investment returns, investment expenses, or administrative fees. N/A = Not applicable.

[a]The IRA scenario reflects maximum allowable contributions (including the catch-up limit for those age 50 and older) to a traditional IRA. Individuals may contribute to a traditional IRA, a Roth IRA or both, but the total annual IRA contribution for all IRAs cannot exceed the lesser of the annual amount or total taxable compensation. For a Roth IRA, the maximum contributions for 1998 to 2011 would be $57,000.

[b]This scenario reflects the upper bound on annual contributions (including the catch-up limit for those age 50 and older) to a single employer DC plan. Our prior work has shown that few contribute at this level in any given year. For example, about one-tenth of one percent of DC plan participants contributed at or above the combined employer-employee contribution limit for 2010.

To illustrate how much an individual could accumulate under each scenario, we reviewed historical stock returns, specifically the Standard & Poor's 500 broad stock index return. Intended to illustrate possible accumulations based on the upper bounds on contributions, the two contribution scenarios assuming 100 percent investment in the stock market are not intended to represent how individuals typically choose to invest. As shown in table 7, we also looked at a range of other possible asset allocations: (1) a 70-percent investment in the S&P 500 and a 30- percent investment in corporate bonds; (2) a glide path starting with a 70- percent investment in the

S&P 500 and a 30-percent investment in corporate bonds, and shifting over time to end with a 30-percent investment in the S&P 500 and a 70-percent investment in corporate bonds; (3) a 30-percent investment in the S&P 500 and a 70-percent investment in corporate bonds; and (4) a 100-percent investment in corporate bonds. For the asset allocations with a mix of stocks and bonds, the portfolio was rebalanced annually. We also calculated the DC contribution scenario with investment returns equal to historical interest rates reported by the Social Security trustees for special-issue government bonds as a proxy for an accumulation with a less aggressive investment allocation.[7] The scenarios do not reflect any investment or administrative fees and expenses.[8] Likewise, the scenarios do not reflect any leakage from withdrawals or employer plan loans over the period.[9] We also calculated the rate of return necessary to accumulate a balance of $1 million or $5 million under each scenario.

Table 7. Alternate Asset Allocation Assumptions and Ending Balances for the Maximum Combined Employer-Employee Contribution Scenario, 1980-2011

Asset allocation	Ending balance ($millions)
100 percent S&P 500 stock investment	7.27
Mix of 70 percent S&P 500 and 30 percent in corporate bonds [a]	7.88
Glide path starting with 70-percent investment in the S&P 500 and 30-percent investment in corporate bonds, and shifting over time to end with 30-percent investment in the S&P 500 and 70 percent investment in corporate bonds [a]	8.59
Mix of 30 percent S&P 500 and 70 percent in corporate bonds [a]	7.74
100 percent investment in corporate bonds	7.08
Investment returns equal to historical interest rates for Social Security	3.38

Source: GAO analysis. | GAO-15-16.

Note: This scenario reflects the upper bound on annual contributions (including the catch-up limit for those age 50 and older) to a single employer DC plan. Our prior work has shown that few contribute at this level in any given year. For example, about one-tenth of one percent of DC plan participants contributed at or above the combined employer-employee contribution limit for 2010.

[a]For the asset allocations with a mix of stocks and bonds, the portfolio was rebalanced annually.

How IRAs Can Become Large

To examine how IRA balances can become large, we conducted literature reviews on IRA investment strategies and held semistructured interviews with more than 60 finance industry stakeholders, government officials, and academics. We conducted initial literature reviews on general topics and key words related to IRAs, contribution limits, and tax policy. We selected a first round of interviewees from these literature reviews and from referrals from GAO stakeholders who have conducted work on retirement, finance, and tax policy. We sought referrals for additional interviews from our first round of interviewees, as well as from more targeted literature reviews based on our initial reviews.

We also searched for documentary evidence of the IRA investment strategies we identified through our interviews and literature reviews. We could not determine IRA investment strategies from IRS data because the IRS does not collect data on asset types held in IRAs. Given this limitation, we searched publicly available filings with the Securities and Exchange Commission, such as the Form S-1 filed by companies seeking to conduct an initial public offering of their stock on public markets, to research the number of nonpublicly traded shares beneficially owned by directors, executive officers, and holders of more than five percent of any class of the company's voting securities. These individuals often comprise the company's founders. We also searched publicly available Form 5500 filings with the Department of Labor (DOL) for the employer-sponsored DC retirement plans of selected private equity firms and hedge funds, primarily 401(k) and profit sharing plans. Specifically, we searched the filings of private equity firms and hedge funds that (1) reported holding partnership interests; (2) are members of the Private Equity Growth Capital Council, an advocacy, communications, and research organization and resource center for the private equity industry; or (3) are cited in the Forbes list of the highest earning hedge fund managers and traders of 2013. The findings of this analysis cannot be generalized to the entire population of private equity firms and hedge funds operating in the United States but provides insights into one potential alternate strategy for accumulating large IRAs.

Our framework for evaluating the performance of tax expenditures draws on long-standing criteria we have described—economic efficiency, equity, simplicity, transparency, and administrability—that can be used to evaluate tax policy.[10] In our review, we focus primarily on (1) the extent to which strategies a few individuals may use to accumulate large IRA balances align with the intended purpose of IRAs; (2) whether tax treatment of individuals who may engage in these strategies is fair and equitable, and (3) the consequences for the federal budget of these IRA strategies.

To provide context for how certain types of nonpublicly traded shares and partnership interests can generate IRA balances of tens of millions of dollars, we constructed two examples. The first example demonstrates how a company founder can invest in nonpublicly traded shares of a newly created company using an IRA, and how these nonpublicly traded shares can grow in value if the company raises capital from outside investors and becomes a publicly traded corporation. The second example demonstrates how a key employee at a private equity firm can invest in a particular type of partnership interest called a profits interest using an IRA or DC plan, and how these profits interests can grow in value if the private investment partnership is successful.

Assessing IRS Enforcement

To assess IRS's examinations of IRA rules and provisions, we developed criteria for evaluating an enforcement program on IRAs. Generally, the basis for the criteria included relevant laws and our previous work on tax administration and policy as well as our previous work and other organizations' work on good management practices.[11] From our research, we concluded that the seven criteria in table 7 were appropriate. We shared the criteria with IRS examination officials. In response to the officials' comments, we considered potential resource and budget limitations in applying the criteria.

To apply the criteria, we collected documentation on IRS enforcement procedures, such as relevant sections of the *Internal Revenue Manual* and other IRS publications on guidance for IRA compliance. We also interviewed relevant IRS enforcement officials with Small Business/SelfEmployed (SB/SE); Wage and Investment (W&I); the SB/SE Lead Development Center; Large Business and International Global High Wealth industry; National Research Program; IRS Chief Counsel; Research, Analysis and Statistics; Estate and Gift Tax; and Tax Forms and Publications. We then compared the findings of our research with the criteria. Table 8 summarizes our determination of how IRS performed on the criteria.

Table 8. Criteria for Assessing Individual Retirement Account Enforcement

Criteria	Basis of criteria	Criteria addressed if …	Summary of thebasis for assessment
Enforcement should cover key IRA laws.	- IRS is charged with enforcing tax laws, and the laws on IRA contributions, distributions, rollovers, and conversions are part of its responsibility.	IRS shows evidence that it operates programs that can address these laws, as shown by program procedures or other documentation. In applying this criterion, we will consider the importance IRS gives to IRA issues relative to other enforcement concerns, given resource limitations.	- W&I's automated underreporter program checks for compliance with contributions and distributions using matching of taxpayer and third-party filings.
			- SB/SE's Abusive Tax and Technical Issues (ATTI) program examines activity that may not comply with IRA laws. - SB/SE conducts field examinations, which can cover IRAs, according to the IRS's Internal Revenue Manual for all examinations.
			- IRS has or has had special compliance projects targeting specific aspects of IRA noncompliance, such as for conversions and rollovers.
			-We also considered indirect activitythat may surface in other units but doesnot specifically target IRAs, such asIRS's Global High Wealth industry and its estate tax enforcement program.

Table 8. (Continued)

Criteria	Basis of criteria	Criteria addressed if …	Summary of thebasis for assessment
Enforcement procedures should take into account the cumulative tax-revenue effect of an improperly valued asset that the taxpayer contributed to a plan.	- IRAs may gain value over time. What starts as small noncompliance may grow into large noncompliance over the life of the investment.	Examination procedures or guidance direct examination staff to review the value of an IRA investment at the time a contribution is made and if examiners have guidance or assistance for determining the value of an asset in an IRA.	- IRS examiner guidance generally instructs staff on reviewing valuation. - SB/SE job aides on IRAs instruct examiners to review valuation. - Engineering Department provides examination with assistance on valuation issues. Examiner guidance directs examiners to use Engineering Department for assistance. - IRS is limited in looking back on IRA issues because of the 3-year statute of limitations.
Enforcement management should collect and use data that will enable examiners to accurately weigh the noncompliance risk of potentially misreported IRA values.	-GAO/AIMD-00-21.3.1, Standards for Internal Control in the Federal Government. In particular, that information should be recorded and communicated to management and other who need it in a form and within a time frame that enables them to carry out their responsibilities.	IRS designs forms to enable the collection of data from tax forms that classifiers and examiners could use to efficiently and accurately determine whether a particular return is at risk of violating the key IRA rules described in the first criterion.	- IRS collects information from custodians on IRA fair market values, rollovers, and conversions from Forms 5498 and 1099-R. - Starting in tax year 2014 and required for 2015, custodians are to report information on IRA asset types, which will help show what types of assets an IRA contains and help examiners weigh the risk of noncompliance. Plans to fully compile and digitize the information from both electronic and paper-filed returns have not been finalized.

Criteria	Basis of criteria	Criteria addressed if …	Summary of thebasis for assessment
	- Our 2012 guide for evaluating tax expenditures, GAO-13-167SP, stating that tax expenditures should be "simple, transparent, and administrable."		
IRAs should be considered in making enforcement plans.	- Office of Management and Budget Circular A-11, on strategic planning, particularly on how executives should use the Strategic Plan to provide guidance to agency components for planning their program implementation.	IRS documentation shows that IRS describes IRAs in strategic planning documents such as its budget, strategic plan, division program letter, or similar planning tools.. The criterion also could be addressed if IRS uses relevant data (such as examination results), if available, in making decisions about and allocating resources for IRA enforcement.	- IRS explicitly has emphasized IRAs as an examination priority in multiple, agency-wide planning documents. For example, IRS's Fiscal Year 2015 budget describes the soft-notice tests for encouraging compliances with IRAs, an initiative to address prohibited transactions in IRAs, and requests increased funds for enforcement of employee retirement plans, which can be rolled into IRAs.
			- Other IRS strategic priorities could overlap with IRA compliance. For example, IRS's strategic plan mentions tax exempt retirement programs and financial instruments, which can feed into IRAs.

Table 8. (Continued)

Criteria	Basis of criteria	Criteria addressed if ...	Summary of thebasis for assessment
			- The Department of the Treasury also lists as priorities enforcement on early distributions from retirement plans and offering additional guidance to facilitate rollovers and other issues relating to lifetime income from retirement plans.
			- IRS has a service-wide process for assessing the risk of emerging issues, which may include IRA noncompliance. As part of this process, IRS developed a task team to study and make recommendations on how to better conduct enforcement on IRA noncompliance. The task team included representation from across IRS.
			- IRS examination management uses data to manage its workload, including the Lead Development Center database. Through this kind of data, IRS could measure progress toward goals, such as examination rates and tax changes.

Criteria	Basis of criteria	Criteria addressed if …	Summary of thebasis for assessment
Examiners should be trained to identify IRA potential compliance issues.	- GAO framework on training, GAO-04-546G.	Examiner training and guidance materials cover the key IRA rules identified in the first criterion, as well as the cumulative effect of long-term IRA noncompliance.	- Training modules for new examiners covers IRA issues. - Examiners job aides provide direction on examining IRA issues. - New continuing professional education training covers prohibited transactions related to IRAs.
IRS should collaborate with the appropriate agency on enforcing laws on certain prohibited transactions that could lead to large, noncompliant IRAs.	- GAO framework for collaboration in GAO-06-15 and GAO-12-1022.	IRS shows documentation on how the agencies have agreed on an approach to share information and interpretations or rulings related to prohibited transactions that could lead to large IRAs.	- For employer plans, IRS has a memorandum of understanding with DOL setting out procedures for collaborating and coordinating in carrying out their joint oversight of prohibited transactions. For IRAs, IRS and DOL officials agreed that they have a good working relationship in their informal consultation process.
			- IRS is working on procedures to streamline its interaction with DOL, building off fact patterns similar to those in Peek v. Commissioner. IRS officials said they have kept DOL informed about their plans.

Table 8. (Continued)

Criteria	Basis of criteria	Criteria addressed if …	Summary of thebasis for assessment
Examination management should collaborate with its own service and outreach functions to help the public better understand laws related to potential IRA investment.	- IRS strategic plan and examination plan. - Project Management Institute standards.	IRS shows that procedures are in place for the examination and service functions to help inform each other about IRA compliance issues. Additionally, current guidance should reflect the issues identified in examination.	- W&I has conducted tests sending letters to certain taxpayers warning them of possible noncompliance. -IRS has a pamphlet warning taxpayers to be aware of IRA schemes.
			- IRS made IRA noncompliance one of its "Dirty Dozen Tax Scams" most recently in 2011.
			- IRS publishes guidance directed at custodians or tax professionals to help encourage compliance with IRA rules.
			This guidance can go beyond simply filling out the lines on IRA information forms. For example, the 5498/1099-R instructions caution that investing in "nonmarketable securities (i.e. alternative assets) raises compliance risks.

Criteria	Basis of criteria	Criteria addressed if …	Summary of thebasis for assessment
			- Prohibited transaction rules, which are complex rules even for pension plan sponsors and their service providers, are covered on irs.gov and discussed in *Publication 590 Individual Retirement Arrangements (IRAs). However,* guidance in Publication 590 does not explicitly caution taxpayers that nonpublic IRA assets are more susceptible to prohibited transactions than publicly traded assets.
			- An ATTI team meets quarterly to address new or potentially new issues that could pose a compliance risk. If the issue is appropriate for outreach, the team contacts the correct office.

Source: GAO analysis. | GAO-15-16.

We used statistics from several databases in our work on assessing IRS enforcement, including the Audit Information Management System, Examination Operational Automation Database, Publication 6961 data, Information Return Program Case Analysis System, and Lead Development Center database. To ensure the data's reliability, we reviewed documentation on the databases and, where necessary, interviewed agency officials. We determined that these data were sufficiently reliable for the purposes of this report.

We conducted this performance audit from June 2013 through October 2014 in accordance with generally accepted government auditing standards. Those standards require that we plan and perform the audit to obtain sufficient, appropriate evidence to provide a reasonable basis for our findings and conclusions based on our audit objectives. We believe that the evidence obtained provides a reasonable basis for our findings and conclusions based on our audit objectives.

Appendix II: Illustration of Earnings and Tax Effects of Traditional and Roth Individual Retirement Accounts

Figure 10 shows the benefits a taxpayer might receive for investing in a tax-advantaged traditional or Roth individual retirement account (IRA) compared to taxable account or investments, given certain assumptions in four different types of investments: a traditional IRA, a Roth IRA, an investment or account that is taxed annually at ordinary income tax rates, and an investment that is subject to capital gains tax rules. The figure uses a simplified model to show the after-tax rates of return that result from these scenarios over a 20-year period.[1] Each case assumes earnings of $1,000 before taxes for contribution in year 1 and distribution of the accumulated balance in year 20. Investment earnings over the 20 year period are assumed to be a constant pretax 5 percent. Assuming a constant federal ordinary income tax rate of 25 percent, the traditional IRA and Roth IRA achieve similar results although the tax benefits have different paths. For the traditional IRA, the individual can invest a $1,000 tax-deductible contribution in year 1, and taxes on the contribution and investment earnings are deferred until distribution. For the Roth IRA, the individual can invest $750 after tax with investment earnings tax-exempt at later distribution. While the amount contributed to the account is greater in the first year for the traditional IRA owner, the amount that is available for the taxpayer for consumption after taxes on distribution is the same for the traditional owner and the Roth owner.

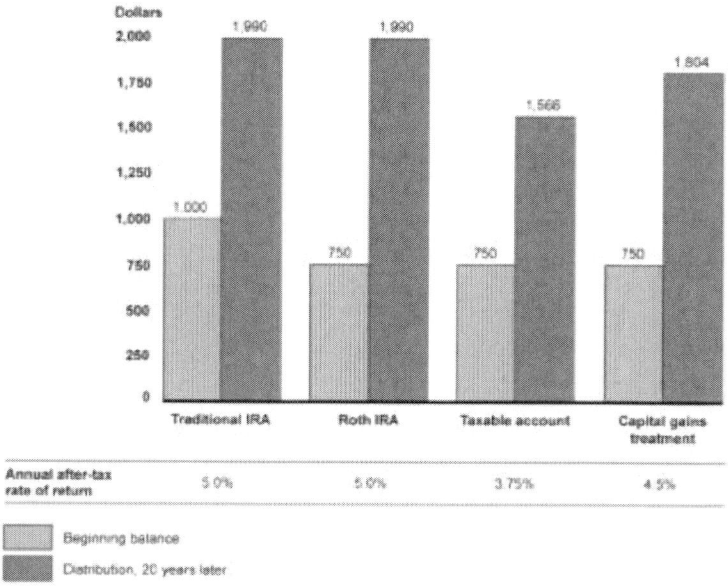

Source: GAO analysis. | GAO-15-16.

Notes: Assumptions include a constant pre-tax rate of return on investment of 5 percent and a tax rate on ordinary income of 25 percent, no distributions until year 20, and the taxpayer is not subject to 10 percent early withdrawal additional tax in year 20.

[a]For $1,000 in earnings pretax, the individual is assumed to make a tax-deductible contribution of $1,000 to the traditional IRA. For the Roth IRA, the income taxable account, and the capital gains treatment, the individual contributes $750 after taxes.

Figure 10. Beginning and After-Tax Ending Balances for $1,000 in Pre-Tax Earnings in a Traditional IRA, Roth IRA and Taxable Accounts over a 20-Year Period.[a]

The traditional IRA owner puts the tax saving in the account to grow to ultimately pay the tax on the account; the Roth owner pays the tax upfront and has no further tax liability. For both Roth and traditional IRA accounts, the after-tax rate of return is 5 percent. In contrast, the taxable account, which is subject to taxes on both the original earnings contributed as well as the annual investment earnings, has an annual after-tax rate of return of 3.75 percent. If an investment were held outside of a retirement account and subject to capital gains taxes only, there would be no initial deduction of amounts invested. Similar to the case of a traditional IRA account where tax on income is deferred until distribution, no capital gains tax would be owed until the asset was sold and gain was realized, which in the example happens at the end of the 20-year period. Upon sale, any gain would be subject to the capital gains tax rate. The capital gains tax rate is generally lower than the ordinary income tax rate that is applied to distributions from a traditional IRA. As a result of the deferral of tax until sale and the preferential capital gains tax rate, the after-tax rate of return for the capital gains asset would be 4.5 percent, less than if the asset were held in an IRA of either type but higher than if the investment had been made in a taxable account where income earned was taxed annually at ordinary income tax rates.

The simplified example above showed how contributions to traditional and Roth accounts can earn the same rate of return after taxes if tax rates do not change over time. If tax rates vary over time, this equivalence may not hold. For example, if an individual or household is subject to a relatively high tax rate when a contribution is made and a low tax rate when earnings are distributed, a traditional account would result in a higher rate of return. On the other hand, if tax rates are low when a contribution to a Roth account is made and rates are higher when funds are distributed, the Roth account would result in a higher rate of return.[2]

APPENDIX III: TABLES FROM STATISTICS OF INCOME DATA FOR TAX YEAR 2011

This appendix shows the confidence intervals for our analysis of the Statistics of Income (SOI) data about individual retirement accounts (IRA).

Table 9. Estimated Median IRA Balances by Size of Individual Retirement Account (IRA) Balance, Tax Year 2011*

IRA Balance	Estimated median IRA balance ($1,000)	95% confidence interval	
Total Taxpayer with IRAs	36	35	36
$1 Million or Less	34	33	35
Greater than $1 million to $2 million	1,282	1,258	1,311
Greater than $2 million to $3 million	2,303	2,235	2,362
Greater than $3 million to $5 million	3,618	3,521	3,658
Greater than $5 million to $10 million	6,044	5,782	6,455
Greater than $10 million to $25 million	12,073	11,469	12,559
Greater than $25 million	69,237	26,822	418,573

Source: GAO analysis of IRS data from Forms 1040, U.S. Individual Income Tax Returns; Forms 5498 IRA Contribution Information. | GAO-15-16.

*Notes: The taxpayer, as a taxpaying unit, may have more than one IRA owner. The IRA balance is the aggregate value for all IRAs (including inherited IRAs) associated with the taxpayer. We assumed the blank IRA fair market values are zero; the blank values could affect these estimates considerably. See appendix I for more details.

Table 10. Estimated Percent of Taxpayers with Individual Retirement Account (IRA) Balances of $1 Million or Less and More Than $5 Million and IRA Balances by Adjusted Gross Income, Tax Year 2011*

IRA balance	Adjusted gross income	Estimated percent of taxpayers	95% confidence interval	
$1 Million or less	0 or less	1.5	1.4	1.6
	$1 to $20,000	13.3	13.0	13.6
	$20,001 to $50,000	24.0	23.6	24.4
	$50,001 to $100,000	32.0	31.6	32.4
	$100,001 to $200,000	21.2	20.9	21.5
	$200,001 to $500,000	6.5	6.4	6.6
	$500,001 to $1,000,000	1.0	1.0	1.1
	Greater than $1,000,000	0.5	0.5	0.5
Greater than $5 Million	0 or less	a**	a**	a**
	$1 to $20,000	a**	a**	a**
	$20,001 to $50,000	a**	a**	a**
	$50,001 to $100,000	2.7	0.5	13.6
	$100,001 to $200,000	4.2	0.9	17.8
	$200,001 to $500,000	35.6	25.2	47.5
	$500,001 to $1,000,000	25.9	18.5	35.0
	Greater than $1,000,000	29.4	23.4	36.3

Source: GAO analysis of IRS data from Forms 1040, U.S. Individual Income Tax Returns; Forms 5498 IRA Contribution Information.| GAO-15-16.

*Notes: The taxpayer, as a taxpaying unit, may have more than one IRA owner. The IRA balance is the aggregate value for all IRAs (including inherited IRAs) associated with the taxpayer. We assumed the blank IRA fair market values are zero; the blank values could affect these estimates considerably.

See appendix I for more details. We do not report on taxpayers with IRA balances greater than $1 million to $5 million to avoid disclosure of taxpayer information.

**aEstimates suppressed due to small cell counts.

Table 11. Estimated Percent of Total IRA Balances by Size of IRA Balance, by Adjusted Gross Income, Tax Year 2011

IRA balance	Adjusted gross income	Estimated percent of total IRA balances	95% confidence interval	
$1 Million or less	0 or less	1	1	1
	$1 to $20,000	7	7	8
	$20,001 to $50,000	16	15	17
	$50,001 to $100,000	31	30	31
	$100,001 to $200,000	29	28	29
	$200,001 to $500,000	12	12	13
	$500,001 to $1,000,000	2	2	3
	Greater than $1,000,000	1	1	1
Greater than $5 Million	0 or less	a**	a**	a**
	$1 to $20,000	a**	a**	a**
	$20,001 to $50,000	a**	a**	a**
	$50,001 to $100,000	2	b***	5
	$100,001 to $200,000	2	b***	5
	$200,001 to $500,000	63	27	99
	$500,001 to $1,000,000	11	b***	23
	Greater than $1,000,000	20	0	39

Source: GAO analysis of IRS data from Forms 1040, U.S. Individual Income Tax Returns; Forms 5498 IRA Contribution Information.| GAO-15-16.

*Notes: The taxpayer, as a taxpaying unit, may have more than one IRA owner. The IRA balance is the aggregate value for all IRAs (including inherited IRAs) associated with the taxpayer. We assumed the blank IRA fair market values are zero; the blank values could affect these estimates considerably. See appendix I for more details. We do not report on taxpayers with IRA balances greater than $1 million to $5 million to avoid disclosure of taxpayer information.

**[a]Estimates suppressed due to small cell counts.

***[b]The distributions for these estimates are so skewed that the usual estimation methods do not produce an accurate lower bound.

APPENDIX IV: EXAMPLES OF STRATEGIES TO ACCUMULATE LARGE INDIVIDUAL RETIREMENT ACCOUNTS

The two examples below demonstrate how a small number of individuals could generate large individual retirement account (IRA) balances by leveraging their access to nonpublicly traded shares and profits interests.

Example 1: Nonpublicly Traded Shares

Figure 11 illustrates an example of how founders of successful companies can generate IRA balances of tens of millions dollars by investing in nonpublicly traded shares in their newly created company. The example is based on Securities and Exchange Commission (SEC) filings detailing the transactions of a technology company founder and assumes the following:[1]

- In 2008, the founders of a newly created company authorize the issuance of up to 100 million shares with an initial value of $0.00125 per share.[2]
- One company founder opens a Roth IRA with an after-tax contribution of $5,000, and uses the Roth IRA to purchase 4 million nonpublicly traded shares in the company.
- The following year, the company raises money by selling nonpublicly traded shares to a private equity fund that focuses on venture capital opportunities (venture capital firm) for $10 per share. As part of this transaction, the company founder sells 1,000,000 shares from her Roth IRA. The founders stipulate that they will retain an "additional consideration" in these shares if the outside investors can someday sell them for more than $30 per share. Specifically, the company founder will receive 20 percent of the profits above $30 per share.
- In 2012, the company offers shares to outside investors through an initial public offering of shares at a price of $25 per share.
- By 2014, the company has enjoyed continuing success and its shares trade on public stock exchanges at $60 per share. The founder retires and sells the remaining shares in her Roth IRA. Additionally, the outside investors of the venture capital firm sell the shares they purchased in 2009 for $60 per share.

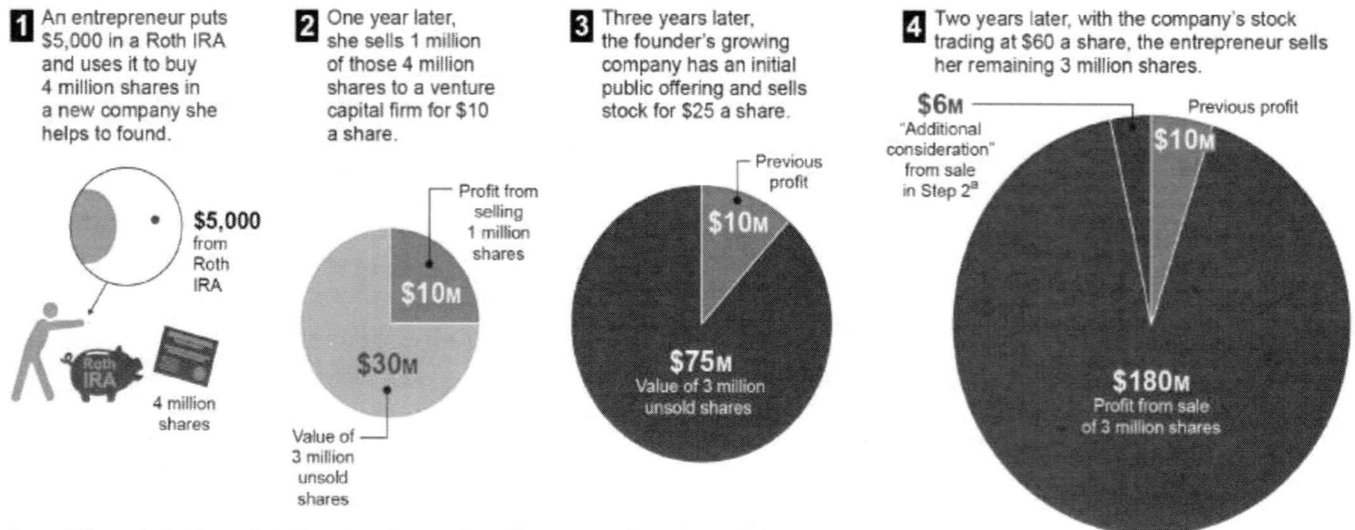

Source: GAO analysis of publicly available filings with the U.S. Securities and Exchange Commission (SEC). | GAO-15-16

[a]In 2009, as part of an effort to raise money for the company, the founder sells 1 million shares of nonpublicly traded shares from her Roth IRA to outside investors at a price of $10 per share. The founders stipulate that they will retain an additional consideration in these shares—specifically, 20 percent of the profits above $30 per share—if the outside investors can someday sell them for more than $30 per share. In 2014, the outside investors sell their now publicly traded shares for $60 per share and get $60 million, $30 million of which is subject to the founder's additional consideration. As a result, the founder realizes a profit of $6 million from the outside investors' sale.

Figure 11. Founders Can Accumulate Large IRAs with Nonpublicly Traded Shares in Their Company.

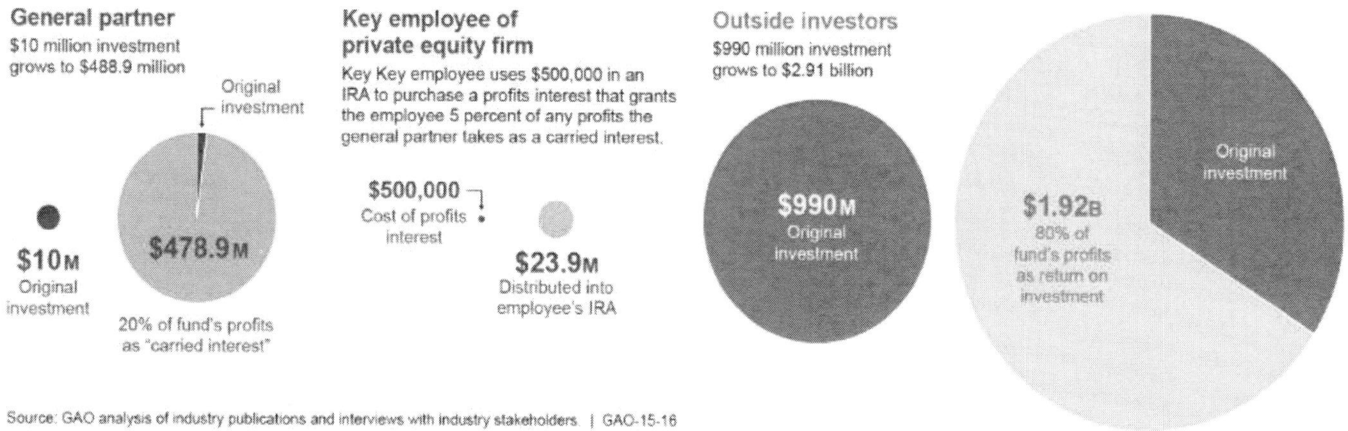

Figure 12. Key Employees of Private Equity Firms Can Accumulate Large Individual Retirement Accounts (IRA) with Profits Interests.

Table 12. Summary of Holdings and Transactions in Company Founder's Roth Individual Retirement Account (IRA)

Year	Description	Amount
2008	Founder contributes to a Roth IRA Nonpublicly traded shares issued by company, initial value per share Number of shares founder purchases using funds in Roth IRA	$5,000 $0.00125 4 million
2009	Number of nonpublicly traded shares sold to outside investors from Roth IRA Sale price of nonpublicly traded shares to outside investors, per share Founder's proceeds from sale Potential value of remaining shares in Roth IRA, based on sale price	1 million $10 $10 million $30 million
2012	Sale price of publicly traded shares in initial public offering, per share Potential value of remaining shares in Roth IRA, based on initial public offering	$25 $75 million
2014	Number of remaining shares founder sells from Roth IRA on public exchanges Founder's proceeds from sale of publicly traded shares Founder's proceeds from additional consideration in outside investors' sale of publicly traded shares Total Assets in founder's Roth IRA at the end of 2014	3 million $180 million $6 million $196 million

Source: GAO analysis of publicly available filings with the U.S. Securities and Exchange Commission. | GAO-15-16.

Example 2: Profits Interest

Figure 12 illustrates an example of how a key employee of a private equity firm can generate an IRA balance of tens of millions of dollars by investing in a profits interest that gives him or her the right to a portion of the general partner's carried interest in a successful fund. The example assumes the following about a general partner entity consisting of 10 key employees:

- In 2004, the general partner of a private equity firm that focuses on buy-out opportunities contributes $10 million to start a new $1 billion buy-out fund.[3] The general partner raises the rest of the capital needed to start the fund from outside investors, known as limited partners.
- The general partner negotiates a performance target that needs to be met in order to get paid for managing the fund. If the general partner meets this performance target, the limited partners pay the general

partner a performance fee equal to 20 percent of the fund's total profits, called the general partner's carried interest in the fund.[4]

- One key employee of the private equity firm rolls over $500,000 from a former employer's 401(k) plan to an IRA and uses it to purchase a profits interest in the general partner. In exchange, the general partner will distribute 5 percent of its carried interest to the key employee if the fund is successful.
- The general partner and key employees successfully invest in portfolio companies over a 10-year period and exceed the performance target set for the limited partners.
- On the last day of the fund, the general partner distributes initial contributions and 80 percent of the fund's profits to the limited partners.[5]
- The general partner retains its initial contributions and 20 percent of the fund's profits as a carried interest. The general partner then distributes 5 percent of this carried interest to the key employee's IRA.

Table 13. Summary of Contributions and Distributions from a $1 Billion Private Equity Fund

Year	Description	Amount
2004	General partner's contribution to the fund	$10 million
	Outside investors' contribution to the fund	$990 million
	Beginning fund balance	$1 billion
2014	Profits from investments in portfolio companies	$2.4 billion
	Initial contributions	$1.0 billion
	Ending fund balance	3.4 billion
2014	Limited partners get:	
	Their initial contribution back	$990 million
	80 percent of the fund's profits	$1.92 billion
	Total distribution to limited partners	$2.91 billion
2014	General partner gets:	
	Their initial contribution back	$10 million
	20 percent of the fund's profits as a carried interest	$478.9 million
	Total distribution to general partner	$488.9 million
2014	The key employee's IRA receives a distribution of 5 percent of the general partner's carried interest	$23.9 million

Source: GAO analysis of industry publications and interviews with industry stakeholders. | GAO-15-16.

APPENDIX V: EXPANDED FIGURE 9 ON FORM 5498

The figure below is an expanded version of figure 9 found earlier in the report.

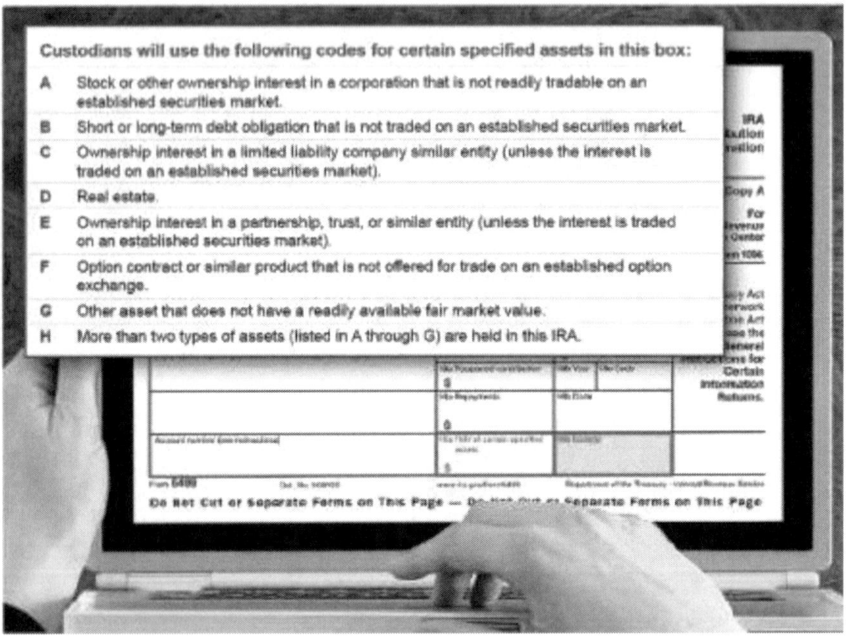

Source: GAO summary of IRS information, PhotoDisc and IRS (images). | GAO-15-16.

Figure 9. Types of Assets Individual Retirement Account Custodians Will Identify on Form 5498 Starting in Tax Year 2014.

End Notes

[1] U.S. retirement assets generally are composed of assets in IRAs, defined contribution plans, defined benefit plans, and annuity at life insurance companies. Board of Governors of the Federal Reserve System, *Financial Accounts of the Untied States: Flow of Funds, Balance Sheets, and Integrated Macroeconomic Accounts First Quarter 2014* (June 5, 2014). Also see, Victoria L. Bryant and Jon Gober, "Accumulation and Distribution of Individual Retirement Arrangements," *2010 Statistics of Income Bulletin* (Fall 2013).

[2] See Office of Management and Budget, *Fiscal Year 2015 Analytical Perspectives: Budget of the U.S. Government* (Washington, D.C.: 2014). The revenue loss is measured as the tax

revenue that the government does not currently collect on contributions and earnings amounts, offset by the taxes paid by those who are currently receiving retirement benefits. The Joint Committee on Taxation (JCT) estimates that IRAs will result in about $17.6 billion in revenue losses in 2014. Revenue loss estimates do not represent the amount of revenue that would be gained from repealing a tax expenditure because repeal would probably change taxpayer behavior in some way that would affect revenue. Treasury also estimates that the present value of the revenue effects (net of future tax payments) from exclusions on traditional IRA contributions and earnings, Roth earnings and distributions, and nondeductible IRA earnings for calendar year 2013 was $1.7 billion, $3.4 billion, and $150 million respectively.

[3] Under the U.S. Bankruptcy Code, a debtor may be able to exempt from the federal bankruptcy estate funds in an IRA up to a certain limit indexed for inflation. 11 U.S.C. § 522(d)(12) and (n). That limit was increased to $1,245,475 in February 2013.

[4] GAO, *Individual Retirement Accounts: Government Actions Could Encourage More Employers to Offer IRAs to Employees*, GAO-08-590 (Washington, D.C.: June 4, 2008) and *Private Pensions: Some Key Features Lead to an Uneven Distribution of Benefits*, GAO-11-333 (Washington, D.C.: Mar. 30, 2011).

[5] GAO, *Understanding the Tax Reform Debate: Background, Criteria, & Questions*, GAO-05-1009SP (Washington, D.C.: September 2005). This report describes how the criteria can be used to evaluate tax policy. In developing the report, we relied on government studies, academic articles, and the advice of tax experts to provide us with information on the issues surrounding the tax reform debate.

[6] GAO, *Tax Expenditures: Background and Evaluation Criteria and Questions* GAO-13-167SP (Washington, D.C.: Nov. 29, 2012). This guide outlines a series of questions and criteria that can be used to evaluate tax expenditures—reductions in a taxpayer's tax liability that are the result of special exemptions and exclusions from taxation, deductions, credits, deferrals of tax liability, or preferential tax rates. To develop the questions, we reviewed our prior work on tax expenditures, tax reform, results-oriented government, and program evaluation, and interviewed experts in tax policy and program evaluation.

[7] All percentage estimates derived from samples used in this report have 95 percent confidence intervals that are within plus or minus 1 percentage point of the estimates themselves, unless otherwise specified. All other estimates in this report have 95 percent confidence intervals that are within plus or minus 15 percent of the estimates themselves, unless otherwise specified.

[8] Estimates based on the small group of taxpayers we studied may have very wide confidence intervals. Our estimates related to the larger IRA balances are less precise as the number of filers in these categories decreased. About 5 percent of the estimated taxpayers with IRAs had at least one associated IRA with blank FMV information. We treated the blank FMVs as zeros. If these IRAs did not, in fact, have zero balances, they could affect our estimates' upper bound considerably. See appendix I for more details.

[9] For a summary of our equity criterion, see GAO-13-167SP. This report draws on GAO-05-1009SP, which summarizes other criteria that we have reported should be considered in evaluating tax policy. These criteria include economic efficiency as well as simplicity, transparency, and administrability.

[10] For prior audits of IRS enforcement of IRA tax laws, see Treasury Inspector General for Tax Administration (TIGTA), *A Service-wide Strategy Is Needed to Address Growing Noncompliance With Individual Retirement Account Contribution and Distribution Requirements*, 2010-40-043 (Washington, D.C.: Mar. 29, 2010); GAO, *Individual*

Retirement Accounts: Additional IRS Actions Could Help Taxpayers Facing Challenges in Complying with Key Tax Rules, GAO-08-654 (Washington, D.C.: Aug. 14, 2008); and TIGTA, *Individual Retirement Account Contributions and Distributions Are Not Adequately Monitored to Ensure Tax Compliance,* 2008-40-087 (Washington, D.C.: Mar. 28, 2008).

[11] For a simplified illustration of the tax effects of traditional and Roth IRAs, as well as a comparison with a taxable investment account, see appendix II.

[12] Failure to take the required minimum is subject to an excise tax on the IRA owner equal to 50 percent of the required amount not distributed.

[13] Pub. L. No.105-34, § 302, 111 Stat. 788, 825-29 (Aug. 5, 1997) codified as amended at 26 U.S.C. § 408A.

[14] Roth conversions were previously subject to an income limit of $100,000. For conversions in 2010 only, a taxpayer had the choice of reporting converted amounts as taxable income in 2010 or half in 2011 and half in 2012. According to IRS SOI estimates, the amount converted to Roth IRAs rose to an estimated $64.8 billion in 2010, surpassing Roth annual contributions for the first time.

[15] Table 5 in appendix I shows the contribution limits by year.

[16] Employers may also set up payroll deduction IRA programs. Through these programs, individuals may establish either traditional or Roth IRAs, and contribute to these accounts through voluntary deductions from their pay, which are forwarded by the employer to the individual's IRA. See GAO, *Individual Retirement Accounts: Government Actions Could Encourage More Employers to Offer IRAs to* Employees, GAO-08-590 (Washington, D.C.: June 4, 2008).

[17] Pub.L. No. 95-600, § 152, 93 Stat. 2763, 2797-2800 (Nov. 6, 1978) codified as amended at 26 U.S.C. § 408(k).

[18] Pub. L. No. 104-188, § 1421, 110 Stat. 1755, 1792-1800 (Aug. 20, 1996) codified as amended at 26 U.S.C. § 408(p).

[19] For employees who participate in other employer plans during the year, the overall total salary reduction contribution limit for all plans is $17,500 ($23,000 for individuals age 50 or older) in 2014.

[20] Rolling employer retirement balances into an IRA is one of several options available and may not be the best choice depending on an individual's circumstances. See GAO, *401(k) Plans: Labor and IRS Could Improve the Rollover Process for Participants*, GAO-13-30 (Washington, D.C.: Mar. 7, 2013).

[21] S. Rep. No. 93-383 at 4 (1973).

[22] 26 U.S.C. § 415(b)(1). Actuarial assumptions and computations are required to figure these contributions.

[23] 26 U.S.C. § 415(c)(1).

[24] Table 5 in appendix I shows the contribution limits by year.

[25] GAO-13-30.

[26] NonRoth employer plans balances can be rolled into a Roth IRA, and the rollover amount is subject to the same rules for converting a traditional IRA to a Roth IRA.

[27] The Internal Revenue Code establishes requirements that private pension plans must satisfy, including minimum coverage and benefits, to qualify for favorable tax treatment. Employers that sponsor these tax-qualified plans are entitled to a deduction (within limits) for the contributions they make. Contributions are not included in an employee's income until benefits are received. Small employers with fewer than 100 employees may also qualify for a federal tax credit for costs associated with starting a new pension plan.

[28] There is also a statutory limit on the total amount of tax-deductible contributions that an employer may make to certain types of plans.

[29] Assets specifically restricted for IRA investment are life insurance and collectibles, such as artwork, rugs, antiques, metals, gems, stamps, coins, and alcoholic beverages.

[30] Employer plans can also invest in alternative assets. See GAO, *Defined Benefit Pension Plans: Recent Developments Highlight Challenges of Hedge Fund and Private Equity Investing*. GAO-12-324 (Washington, D.C.: Feb. 16, 2012).

[31] Disqualified persons include, for example, an IRA fiduciary, a person providing services, and members of the IRA owner's family (spouse, ancestor, lineal descendant, and any spouse of a lineal descendant). 26 U.S.C. § 4975(e)(2). A fiduciary is anyone who exercises discretionary authority or discretionary control in managing an IRA or exercises any authority or control in managing or disposing of its assets; provides investment advice to an IRA for a fee or has the responsibility to do so; and has any discretionary authority or discretionary responsibility in administering an IRA. 29 U.S.C. § 1002(21).The IRA owner and the IRA's beneficiaries are considered disqualified persons for purposes of the prohibited transaction rules.

[32] 26 U.S.C. § 408(e)(2).

[33] If a disqualified person other than the IRA owner engages in a prohibited transaction, that person may be liable for a 15 percent excise tax on the amount of the prohibited transaction and a 100 percent additional tax if the transaction is not corrected. 26 U.S.C. § 4975(a) and (b).

[34] Treasury regulations define FMV for purposes of valuation of plan assets as "the price at which the property would change hands between a willing buyer and a willing seller, neither being under any compulsion to buy or sell and both having reasonable knowledge of relevant facts." 26 C.F.R. § 1.412(c)(2)-1(c).

[35] IRS also has offices to address criminal activity by taxpayers (Criminal Investigations) and misconduct by certain practitioners (Office of Professional Responsibility) that may overlap with IRA issues but neither of these programs performs examinations on individual income taxes.

[36] See section 102 of the Reorganization Plan No. 4 of 1978 (43 Fed. Reg. 47,713).

[37] For more on IRS's automated matching of IRA transactions reported on tax returns to custodian reporting, see GAO-08-654.

[38] To view the 2014 Form 5498, visit http://www.irs.gov/pub/irs-pdf/f5498.pdf.

[39] To view the 2014 Form 1099-R, visit http://www.irs.gov/pub/irs-pdf/f1099r.pdf.

[40] In 2008, we suggested that Congress expand IRS math error authority to automatically correct tax returns for taxpayers younger than age 50 incorrectly claiming catch up contributions and taxpayers older than age 701/2 improperly deducting IRA contributions. See *GAO, Tax Administration: IRS's 2008 Filing Season Generally Successful Despite Challenges, although IRS Could Expand Enforcement during Returns Processing*, GAO-09-146 (Washington, D.C.: Dec. 12, 2008). Congress has not taken action on this suggestion as of October 2014.

[41] Correspondence examinations are conducted through mail, while field examination, in which IRS meets with taxpayers or the taxpayers' representatives, are done face to face.

[42] Publication 560 explains rules for employer-sponsored SEP and SIMPLE IRA plans in more detail.

[43] We use taxpayer to denote the taxpaying unit including individuals, heads of household, and married couples filing a joint return. IRAs owned by dependents are aggregated with the filer's IRA. Taxpayers included those filing a return but reporting no taxable income— for

example those with incomes below a certain threshold. We report aggregated IRA balances for taxpayers as individuals can own more than one IRA. The aggregate balance includes inherited IRAs, as IRS data do not readily identify inherited IRAs. We estimated taxpayers with IRA balances of $1 million or less had an average of three IRAs whereas those with IRA balances over $5 million had about five to six IRAs on average. We did not include information about IRA owners who did not file an individual income tax return. However we have no evidence from the IRA dataset that there were IRA owners with unusually large IRA balances who did not file an income tax return for 2011.

[44] Both the numbers and percentages have been rounded as some of these estimates may have very wide confidence intervals, particularly estimates related to the fewer taxpayers with larger IRA balances. Additionally, about 5 percent of taxpayers with IRAs had at least one associated IRA with no FMV information, which we treated as zeros. If these IRAs did not, in fact, have zero FMVs, they could affect our estimates' upper bound considerably. See appendix I for more details.

[45] The very large aggregated balances are reflected in the difference between the estimated median and mean FMVs where the median is about a quarter of the mean for this group. The large discrepancy between the median and mean indicates that a small number of taxpayers with very large IRA balances are raising the mean well above the median.

[46] AGI is the individual's gross income minus adjustments to income. These adjustments include deductions for trade or business expenses, losses from the sale or exchange of property, contribution to pensions and other retirement, as well as alimony paid. About 1 percent to 2 percent of the taxpayers reported zero AGI. However, to determine eligibility for Roth IRA contributions or deductions for contributions to a traditional IRA, a modified AGI, in which certain items such as foreign housing exclusion and student loan interest deductions are added back to the AGI, is used.

[47] The scenarios illustrate balances accumulated by an individual in an IRA or DC plan. In contrast, for our analysis of IRA balances using SOI estimates, we examined aggregate IRA balances by taxpaying unit. A tax return could include more than one person, such as a married couple filing a joint return.

[48] Both scenarios assume catch-up contributions for those age 50 and older beginning in 2002.

[49] GAO, *Private Pensions: Pension Tax Incentives Update*, GAO-14-334R (Washington, D.C.: Mar. 20, 2014).

[50] Some DB plans allow participants to receive a lump sum payment in place of what would otherwise be regular benefit payments. In 2011, the total limit on an annual DB benefit payment was $195,000.

[51] As discussed further below, IRS plans to collect additional IRA data beginning in 2014.

[52] Other studies we reviewed provided snapshots of IRA asset allocation but did not contain complete information, such as IRAs invested in nonpublicly traded alternative assets held by specialty custodians. See, Holden, Sarah, and Daniel Schrass, "The IRA Investor Profile: Roth IRA Investors' Activity, 2007–2012," *ICI Research Report* (Washington, D.C.: June 2014); Holden, Sarah, and Steven Bass, "The IRA Investor Profile: Traditional IRA Investors' Activity, 2007–2012." *ICI Research Report* (Washington, D.C.: March 2014); and Employee Benefit Research Institute, "IRA Asset Allocation, 2011," *EBRI Notes*, Vol. 34, No. 10 (October 2013).

[53] The Obama Administration in its fiscal year 2014 and 2015 budgets proposed limiting tax deferrals beyond the taxpayer and spouse's lifetime by requiring distribution within 5 years for IRAs inherited by nonspousal beneficiaries. According to Treasury's estimates, the fiscal year 2015 budget proposal would generate an estimated $5.2 billion from 2015

through 2024. JCT estimated that the Administration's 2015 proposal would generate about $5 billion for the same period.

[54] See GAO, *Unemployed Older Workers: Many Experience Challenges Regaining Employment and Face Reduced Retirement Security*, GAO-12-445 (Washington, D.C.: Apr. 25, 2012).

[55] Par value refers to the value initially assigned to a stock or bond when it is issued. Founders of newly created companies register the par value of their nonpublicly traded shares with the state in which they are incorporated. Par value does not necessarily correspond with the price paid, if any, by founders of a company for newly issued nonpublicly traded shares in their company.

[56] SEC defines individual accredited investors in Rule 501(a) of Regulation D as any person who comes within certain categories, or who the issuer of the securities reasonably believes comes within certain categories, at the time of the sale of the securities to that person. Some of these categories include: (i) any director, executive officer, or general partner of the issuer of the securities being offered or sold, or any director, executive officer, or general partner of a general partner of that issuer; (ii) any natural person whose individual net worth, or joint net worth with that person's spouse exceeds $1,000,000 (subject to the provisions in Rule 501(a)(5) regarding how to calculate net worth; for example, the person's primary residence shall not be included as an asset); and (iii) any natural person who had an individual income in excess of $200,000 in each of the two most recent years or joint income with that person's spouse in excess of $300,000 in each of those years and has a reasonable expectation of reaching the same income level in the current year. We found in 2013 that an individual accredited investor is generally an investor who possesses knowledge and experience in finance and business matters to evaluate the risks and merits of prospective investments or one who the issuer of such investments reasonably believes meets this description. See GAO, *Securities and Exchange Commission: Alternative Criteria for Qualifying as An Accredited Investor Should Be Considered*, GAO-13-640 (Washington, D.C.: July 18, 2013). We found in 2008 that most hedge funds restrict their sales to accredited investors, which exempt their offerings from certain registration requirements. See GAO, *Hedge Funds: Regulators and Market Participants Are Taking Steps to Strengthen Market Discipline, but Continued Attention Is Needed*, GAO-08-200 (Washington, D.C.: Jan. 24, 2008).

[57] Specifically, we found that the percentage of large DB plans (as measured by total plan assets) investing in hedge funds grew from 47 percent in 2007 to 60 percent in 2010, while the percentage of large plans investing in private equity increased from 80 percent to 92 percent, in both cases continuing a decade-long upward trend. See GAO, *Defined Benefit Pension Plans: Recent Developments Highlight Challenges of Hedge Fund and Private Equity Investing*, GAO-12-324 (Washington, D.C.: Feb. 16, 2012).

[58] Additionally, investment returns for limited partners, who hold capital interests in a partnership are generally commensurate to the amount they invest. Further, as we found in 2012, large DB plan investments in private equity and hedge funds represent a relatively small percentage of total plan assets. See GAO-12-324. However, these plans' widespread participation in private equity and hedge funds highlights the importance of having transparent information on, among other things, the fees they charge their limited partners. Such information is needed to help plan sponsors carry out their fiduciary responsibilities to participants, such as the requirement to invest with the care, skill, and diligence of a prudent person familiar with such matters. Private sector pension plan investment decisions must comply with ERISA, which includes fiduciary standards based on the principal of a "[p]rudent man standard of care." 29 U.S.C. § 1104. Public sector plans, such as those at the

state, county, and municipal levels, are not subject to most ERISA requirements applicable to private sector pension plans. To receive preferential tax treatment, however, to the extent they operate through a trust format, they must follow IRS requirements applicable to such trusts.

[59] SEC documents indicate that the initial value, or par value, of these nonpublicly traded shares was $0.000001 per share. As a result, the founder could have paid as little as $4 from after-tax contributions to purchase almost 4 million shares. In contrast, from 2000 through June of 2014, companies charged an average of $14.50 per share through initial public offerings, when companies first offer shares to the general public, often primarily to institutional and high net-worth investors. At this price, four million shares would cost an investor about $58 million before commissions or fees, well in excess of annual IRA contribution limits.

[60] According to two industry stakeholders, private equity firms generally use these shares as an incentive to hire and retain managers of the portfolio company, but may also make shares available to their own employees. More recently, private equity funds appear to have been restructuring portfolio companies' shares as stock options rather than splitting them into various classes of nonpublicly traded shares. For example, according to a 2013 PricewaterhouseCoopers (PwC) study of portfolio company compensation, 70 percent of the incentives offered to portfolio company management come in the form of stock options. See PwC: *Driving Portfolio Company Performance in a Changing Private Equity Environment* (2013).

[61] Preferred shares have a higher initial value because holders of this share class are more likely to be repaid if the portfolio company is not successful. Additionally, holders of preferred shares are the first to receive proceeds from the private equity fund's sale of the portfolio company. In contrast, the riskier common shares can end up worthless if the private equity fund sells the portfolio company for less than it paid. But if the portfolio company is sold for a higher price than expected, holders of the riskier common shares may receive the bulk of any additional proceeds once preferred share holders have received their proceeds.

[62] According to two industry stakeholders, private equity firms currently use a ratio of about 4:1 to split the value of a portfolio company between preferred and common share classes, respectively. This means about 80 percent of the company's value would be assigned to the preferred share class and the remainder to the common share class. In some instances in the 1990's, private equity funds used ratios as high as 9:1, which one industry stakeholder said would have been seen as "pushing the envelope" at the time. Another industry stakeholder said that today, a ratio this high would likely be challenged as aggressively devaluing the riskier common share class.

[63] Liquidation value is the value of a business or of an asset when it is sold in liquidation, as opposed to being sold in the ordinary course of business. Liquidation price is usually below the market price.

[64] Mark Maremont, "Bain Gave Staff Way to Swell IRAs by Investing in Deals," *Wall Street Journal,* Mar. 29, 2012 (New York City).

[65] In this report, we refer to private equity firms and hedge funds that are organized as partnerships typically consisting of: (1) a general partner, an entity that is responsible for management of the fund, and; (2) outside investors, commonly referred to as limited partners. Although there is no universally accepted definition of hedge funds, the term is commonly used to describe pooled investment vehicles that are privately organized and often engage in active trading of various types of securities, commodity futures, options contracts, and other investment vehicles. Likewise, there is no commonly accepted definition of private equity funds, but such funds are generally privately managed pools of

capital that invest in companies, many of which are not listed on a stock exchange. Strategies of private equity funds vary, but most funds target either venture capital or buy-out opportunities. Venture capital funds invest in young companies that often are developing a new product or technology. Buy-out funds generally invest in larger established companies and attempt to add value. For both venture capital and buy-out strategies, investors hope to profit when the company is eventually sold, either when offered to the public or when sold to another investor or company. See GAO-12-234 and GAO, *Defined Benefit Pension Plans: Guidance Needed to Better Inform Plans of the Challenges and Risks of Investing in Hedge Funds and Private Equity*, GAO-08-692 (Washington, D.C.: Aug. 14, 2008).

[66] IRS Rev. Proc. 93-27, 1993-27 C.B. 343 and Rev. Proc. 2001-43, 2001-2 C.B. 191.

[67] According to DOL officials, the general partner must meet contractual obligations to contribute cash to the retirement plan before granting profits interests to key employees. DOL spells out rules under which employers can make in-kind contributions, that is, contributions other than cash. 29 C.F.R. § 2509.94-3.

[68] Treasury regulations generally define FMV for the purposes of valuation of plan assets as, "the price at which the property would change hands between a willing buyer and a willing seller, neither being under any compulsion to buy or sell and both having reasonable knowledge of relevant facts." 26 C.F.R. § 1.412(c)(2)-1(c).

[69] For example, in *Campbell v. Commissioner*, the Eighth Circuit Court of Appeals overturned a decision by the U.S. Tax Court and held that an individual who is granted a profits interest does not need to recognize any income if the profits interest does not have a readily ascertainable value. 943 F.2d 815, 823 (8th Cir. 1991).

[70] Generally, IRS has 3 years from the date a return is filed (whether the return is filed on time or not) to make an assessment of tax liability. 26 U.S.C. § 6501(a). The statute of limitations is extended in certain situations. For example, if a taxpayer submits a false or fraudulent tax return or otherwise engages in a willful attempt to evade a tax, the tax may be assessed at any time after the return is filed. 26 U.S.C. § 6501(c)(1), (2). Also, IRS and the taxpayer may agree to extend the statute of limitations for assessment. 26 U.S.C. § 6501(c)(4). Other extensions are authorized when the taxpayer fails to file a tax return, omits a certain amount of gross income from the return, or fails to report a listed transaction. 26 U.S.C. §§ 6501(c)(3), (10) and (e)(1). A listed transaction is a transaction that is the same as, or substantially similar to, one that IRS has determined to be a tax avoidance transaction and identified by IRS notice or other form of published guidance.

[71] See GAO-12-324.

[72] Profit sharing plans and 401(k) plans governed by ERISA and the Internal Revenue Code may generally satisfy annual reporting requirements by filing a *Form 5500 Annual Return/Report of Employee Benefit Plan* (Form 5500) and its accompanying schedules. Plans with 100 or more participants are generally required to file Schedule H (Financial Information) detailing, among other things, information about the plan's assets. Plans filing Schedule H are also generally required to attach the report of an independent qualified public accountant detailing information about the plan and a "Schedule of Assets (Held at End of Year)" listing assets held by the plan. In contrast, plans with less than 100 participants may be eligible to file Schedule I (Financial Information-Small Plan), with less detailed information on plan assets, in place of Schedule H. Also, certain plans with fewer than 100 participants that invest only in eligible assets may file the *Short Form Annual Report/Report of Small Employee Benefit Plan* (Form 5500-SF), which is a simplified annual report form, instead of the Form 5500. Form 5500-SF filers generally are not

required to file schedules or attachments, such as the Schedule H and attached schedule of assets. Employers that offer SEP IRA and SIMPLE IRA plans generally do not have to file Form 5500s.

[73] DOL officials told us that Form 5500-SF filers are prohibited from allowing participants to invest directly in nonpublicly traded shares or profits interests. They said it was conceivable that participants might be able to invest in these types of assets indirectly through the use of Common Collective Trusts, but that this was unlikely. Small plans that directly invest in or allow participants to invest directly in nonpublicly traded shares or profits interests would be required to file the Form 5500 and the Schedule I.

[74] DOL officials reviewed filings for two of the hedge funds and pointed out possible mistakes in the filings. For example, both filers reported that their plan did not hold hardto-value assets, which DOL officials said was unlikely given that assets in both plans were substantially invested in the employer's own funds. Only one of the five filers we reviewed reported holding hard-to-value assets. This raises questions about the possibility that private equity firms and hedge funds, including those that file Form 5000-SF, may not be aware of, or complying with, filing requirements with respect to investments in nonpublicly traded shares and profits interests.

[75] GAO, *Private Pensions: Targeted Revisions Could Improve Usefulness of Form 5500 Information*, GAO-14-441 (Washington, D.C.: June 5, 2014).

[76] We reported that only 12.5 percent of all plans that filed a Form 5500 in 2011 included a Schedule H. See GAO-14-441.

[77] In comments on that report, DOL officials did not say whether they agreed or disagreed with our recommendation, but did identify actions underway to address our recommendation.

[78] Some private equity fund and hedge fund managers will remain exempt from registration with SEC. For example, certain fund managers with less than $150 million in assets under management will not be required to register with the SEC. See Exemptions for Advisers to Venture Capital Funds, Private Fund Advisors with Less than $150 Million in Assets Under Management, and Foreign Private Advisers (final rule), 76 Fed. Reg. 39,646 (July 6, 2011).

[79] Specifically, we interviewed representatives of 22 public and private sector DB plans to determine what steps they had taken, if any, to address the challenges of investing in private equity funds and hedge funds particularly given ongoing market volatility in the years following the financial market events of 2008. The DB plan representatives we contacted took significant steps to improve the terms of their investments, including negotiating lower fees or more advantageous fee terms, and obtaining greater liquidity or transparency. See GAO-12-324.

[80] See S. Rep. No. 93-383 at 27 (1973): H.R. Rep. No. 93-807 at 4 (1974).

[81] 26 U.S.C. §415.

[82] Prior to ERISA, DC plans were often referred to as salary reduction plans. In response to controversy over proposed regulations that would have altered their tax treatment, ERISA effectively froze the tax treatment of such plans in anticipation of more specific legislative action to deal with them. Pub. L. No. 93-406, § 2006, 88 Stat. 829, 992-93 (Sept. 2, 1974). That legislative action came four years later in the form of the Revenue Act of 1978, which created 401(k) plans—now the dominant type of retirement plan offered by private sector employers. But the relevant provision did not take full effect until January 1, 1980. Pub. L. No. 95-600, § 135.92 Stat. 2763, 2785-87 (Nov. 6, 1978).

[83] H.R. Rep. No. 93-807 at 112.

[84] See GAO, *Government Performance and Accountability: Tax Expenditures Represent a Substantial Federal Commitment and Need to Be Reexamined*, GAO-05-690 (Washington,

D.C.: Sep. 23, 2005). Tax expenditures are special tax credits, deductions, exclusions, exemptions, deferrals, and preferential tax rates that can substantially reduce federal tax revenues.

[85] GAO-13-167SP.

[86] The equity criterion also asks whether the tax expenditure results in different benefits for similarly situated taxpayers. Additionally, our framework includes criteria such as how the tax expenditure relates to other federal programs and how evaluation of the tax expenditure should be managed. A review of retirement tax expenditures for DC plans and IRAs should include all aspects of the tax expenditure evaluation framework.

[87] For more details on our methodology, see appendix I.

[88] Internal Revenue Service, "Abusive Roth IRA Transactions," *Internal Revenue Bulletin No. 2004-4*, Notice 2004-8 (Jan. 26, 2004).

[89] "Self-dealing" specifically refers to the prohibited transactions set forth in 26 U.S.C. § 4975(c)(1)(D)-(F).

[90] 26 C.F.R. § 301.6011-2(b)(1). IRS is generally prohibited from requiring those filing less than 250 returns annually from filing electronically. 26 U.S.C.§ 6011(e)(2)(A). Each type of information return is considered a separate return for determining the 250 threshold. 26 C.F.R. § 301.6011-2(c)(1)(iii).

[91] See GAO, *Partnerships and S Corporations: IRS Needs to Improve Information to Address Tax Noncompliance*, GAO-14-453 (Washington, D.C.: May 14, 2014); *Tax Administration: IRS Could Improve Examinations by Adopting Certain Research Program Practices*, GAO-13-480 (Washington, D.C.: May 24, 2013); and *E-Filing Tax Returns: Penalty Authority and Digitizing More Paper Return Data Could Increase Benefits*, GAO-12-33 (Washington, D.C.: Oct. 5, 2011).

[92] See GAO, *IRS 2015 Budget Long-Term Strategy and Return on Investment Data Needed to Better Manage Budget Uncertainty and Set Priorities,* GAO-14-605 (Washington D.C.: June 12, 2014)

[93] Internal Revenue Service, *Calendar Year Projections of Information and Withholding Documents for the United States and IRS Campuses*, Publication 6961 (Washington, D.C.: 2014).

[94] The range is partly attributable to the different transcription systems that IRS could use. A W&I program analyst said that the estimates are for direct costs only and are dependent on programming changes being made to accommodate the record layout for transcription. IRS also estimates that it would cost as much as $38,000 in necessary programming for the transcription.

[95] There is a 6-year statute of limitations for assessment if the taxpayer omits gross income in an amount that exceeds 25 percent of the gross income reflected on the return. Even if a substantial error is identified, the IRS generally will not go back more than the last six years. Also, the clock for the statute of limitations does not begin to run until all required tax returns are filed. As discussed below, IRS has considered legislative action to extend the statute of limitations to 6 years for all IRA activity.

[96] For example, IRS Chief Counsel officials said IRS has not completed an audit in which the founder stock purchase facts were present. DOL retains the ultimate authority to interpret whether such a transaction would constitute a prohibited transaction.

[97] For employer plans, IRS has a memorandum of understanding with DOL established in 2003 setting out procedures for collaborating and coordinating in carrying out their joint oversight of prohibited transactions. An addendum issued in October 2013 added detail to the procedures for communicating and making referrals.

[98] 140 T.C. 216 (2013).

[99] The IMT also suggested changing rules about the duties and role of custodians with respect to appraisals and due diligence. In addition, the IMT suggested exploring custodian penalties either under existing code sections or through new legislation.

[100] This Executive Steering Committee is a forum to develop a unified cross-divisional approach to compliance strategies needing collaboration, including emerging issue and abusive tax avoidance transactions.

[101] According to Treasury's estimates, the Obama Administration's fiscal year 2015 proposal limiting the total accrual for tax-favored retirement benefits would generate an estimated $28.4 billion from 2015 through 2024. However, the Joint Committee on Taxation estimated that the Administration's 2015 proposal would generate about $4.3 billion for a similar period.

[102] GAO-08-654.

[103] IRS, *An Important Message for Taxpayers with IRAs*, Publication 3125 (10-2009), Catalog Number 26091B.

End Notes for Appendix I

[1] All percentage estimates derived from samples used in this report have 95 percent confidence intervals that are within plus or minus 1 percentage point of the estimates themselves, unless otherwise specified. All other estimates in this report have 95 percent confidence intervals that are within plus or minus 15 percent of the estimates themselves, unless otherwise specified.

[2] Estimates based on the small group of taxpayers we studied may have very wide confidence intervals. Our estimates related to the larger IRA balances are less precise as the number of filers in these categories decreased.

[3] The predominant type of defined contribution (DC) plan, the 401(k) plan, became available in 1980. Prior to 1987, DC plans had a single limit on employer and employee contributions. The Tax Reform Act of 1986 imposed a limit on employee deferral contributions, but still maintained the total limit on annual contributions.

[4] An individual with multiple employers could participate in more than one employer DC plan. Also, an individual could roll over a lump sum distribution from an employer DC plan.

[5] GAO, *Private Pensions: Pension Tax Incentives Update*,GAO-14-334R (Washington, D.C.: Mar. 20, 2014); *Private Pensions: Some Key Features Lead to an Uneven Distribution of Benefits*, GAO-11-333 (Washington, D.C.: Mar. 30, 2011); and *Private Pensions: Issues of Coverage and Increasing Contribution Limits for Defined Contribution Plans*, GAO-01-846 (Washington, D.C: Sept. 17, 2001).

[6] For our analysis of IRA balances using SOI estimates, we examined aggregate IRA balances by taxpaying unit. A tax return could include more than one person, such as a married couple filing a joint return.

[7] We previously calculated the IRA contribution scenario showing investment returns equal to historical interest rates reported by the Social Security trustees for special issue government bonds. See GAO, *Individual Retirement Accounts: Preliminary Information on IRA Balances Accumulated as of 2011*, GAO-14-878T (Washington, D.C.: Sept. 16, 2014).

[8] Fees charged for such services as investment management, recordkeeping, consulting, and customer service, can also reduce accumulated savings. GAO, *401(k) Plans: Increased*

Educational Outreach and Broader Oversight May Help Reduce Plan Fees, GAO-12-325 (Washington, D.C.: Apr. 24, 2012). An additional 1 percent annual charge for fees could reduce an individual account balance by 17 percent over a 20 year period. GAO, *Private Pensions: Changes Needed to Provide 401(k) Plan Participants and the Department of Labor Better Information on Fees*, GAO-07-21 (Washington, D.C.: Nov. 16, 2006). DC plan fees can range from an average of 0.15 to 1.33 percent of assets depending on the size of the plan. GAO, *401(k) Plans: Increased Educational Outreach and Broader Oversight May Help Reduce Plan Fees*, GAO-12-325 (Washington, D.C.: Apr. 24, 2012).

[9] As with retirement plans, leakages from IRA accounts may occur when IRA owners use their accumulated savings prior to retirement for nonretirement purposes thereby reducing the accumulated balances. GAO, *401(k) Plans: Policy Changes Could Reduce the Longterm Effects of Leakage on Workers' Retirement Savings*, GAO-09-715 (Washington, D.C.: Aug. 28, 2009).

[10] GAO, *Tax Expenditures: Background and Evaluation Criteria and Questions* GAO-13-167SP (Washington, D.C.: Nov. 29, 2012). This guide outlines a series of questions and criteria that can be used to evaluate tax expenditures—reductions in a taxpayer's tax liability that are the result of special exemptions and exclusions from taxation, deductions, credits, deferrals of tax liability, or preferential tax rates. To develop the questions, we reviewed our prior work on tax expenditures, tax reform, results-oriented government, and program evaluation, and interviewed experts in tax policy and program evaluation. Also, see GAO, *Understanding the Tax Reform Debate: Background, Criteria, & Questions*, GAO-05-1009SP (Washington, D.C.: September 2005). This report describes how the criteria can be used to evaluate tax policy. In developing the report, we relied on government studies, academic articles, and the advice of tax experts to provide us with information on the issues surrounding the tax reform debate.

[11] For prior audits of IRS enforcement of IRA tax laws, see Treasury Inspector General for Tax Administration (TIGTA), *A Service-wide Strategy Is Needed to Address Growing Noncompliance With Individual Retirement Account Contribution and Distribution Requirements*, 2010-40-043 (Washington, D.C.: Mar. 29, 2010); GAO-08-654; and TIGTA, *Individual Retirement Account Contributions and Distributions Are Not Adequately Monitored to Ensure Tax Compliance*, 2008-40-087 (Washington, D.C.: Mar. 28, 2008. See also GAO-13-167SP; *Managing for Results: Key Considerations for Implementing Interagency Collaborative Mechanisms*, GAO-12-1022 (Washington, D.C.: Sept. 27, 2012); *Tax Gap: IRS Could Do More to Promote Compliance by Third Parties with Miscellaneous Income Reporting Requirements*, GAO-09-238 (Washington, D.C.: Jan. 28, 2009); *Results-Oriented Government: Practices That Can Help Enhance and Sustain Collaboration among Federal Agencies*, GAO-06-15 (Washington, D.C.: Oct. 21, 2005); and GAO-05-1009SP.

End Notes for Appendix II

[1] Our model, including the tax and return assumptions, is based on a similar example produced in Brady, Peter. Investment Company Institute, *The Tax Benefits and Revenue Costs of Tax Deferral* (Washington, D.C.: September 2012), as well as a Joint Committee on Taxation (JCT) publication, JCT, *Present Law and Background Relating to the Tax Treatment of Retirement Savings*, JCX-32-12 (Washington, D. C.: Apr. 13, 2012).

[2] For further discussion, see JCT, *Present Law and Background Relating to the Tax Treatment of Retirement Savings*, JCX-32-12, (Washington, D.C.: Apr. 13, 2012), 68-71.

End Notes for Appendix IV

[1] The example is based in part on a filing of SEC Form S-1, which requires disclosure of the number of shares beneficially owned at the time of the offering by directors, executive officers, and holders of more than 5 percent of any class of the company's voting securities. According to SEC officials, disclosure regarding an individual's Roth IRA is not explicitly required on Form S-1.

[2] This example assumes no fees, trading costs, or commissions on transactions.

[3] This contribution establishes the general partner as a partner in the fund and gives the general partner the right to performance fees negotiated with outside investors. These performance fees can be disproportionately larger than general partner's investment if the fund is successful. In other words, the general partner's contribution is to a large extent an investment of key employees' ideas, expertise, and work to make the fund a success rather than an investment of capital. If, on the other hand, the fund is not a success, the general partner may not receive any performance fees. For this reason, the general partner's contribution is referred to as a profits interest in the fund. According to an industry stakeholder. the general partner may also make a larger investment in the fund on the same terms as other outside investors, or limited partners.

[4] This example assumes no fees other than the general partner's carried interest in the fund. For example, private equity firms generally charge fees both to outside investors for managing the fund and to portfolio companies for providing advisory services.

[5] For simplicity, we assume no distributions until the last day of the investment fund. In practice, the timing of distributions varies.

In: Individual Retirement Accounts
Editor: Jake Silva

ISBN: 978-1-63482-176-6

Chapter 2

TESTIMONY OF SCOTT F. BETTS, SENIOR VICE PRESIDENT OF NATIONAL BENEFITS SERVICES, LLC. HEARING ON "RETIREMENT SAVINGS 2.0: UPDATING SAVINGS POLICY FOR THE MODERN ECONOMY"*

Thank you Chairman Wyden, Ranking Member Hatch and members of the Finance Committee for the opportunity to talk with you about our private employer-sponsored retirement system. My name is Scott Betts and I am Senior Vice President of National Benefits Services, LLC (NBS). NBS is a fee-for-service Third Party Administrator specializing in the design and administration of all types of employer-sponsored retirement and benefit plans. NBS has more than 225 employees located in West Jordan, Utah, and supports more than 7,500 retirement and benefit plans in 46 states. I am also a member of the American Society of Pension Professionals and Actuaries (ASPPA). ASPPA is a non-profit professional organization with two major goals: to educate all retirement and benefits professionals like myself, and to advocate for policies that give every working American the ability to save for a comfortable retirement.

I am pleased to report that our private employer-sponsored retirement system in general, and 401(k) plans in particular, have been successful at

* This is an edited, reformatted and augmented version of testimony presented September 16, 2014 before the Senate Finance Committee.

providing substantial retirement benefits for tens of millions of American workers at all income levels. These plans benefit middle class families who represent the overwhelming majority of participants in 401(k) plans: 80 percent of participants in 401(k) plans make less than $100,000 per year, and 43 percent of participants in these plans make less than $50,000 per year (see chart #1).[1] The primary factor in determining whether or not a middle-income worker is saving for retirement is whether or not they have a retirement plan at work. Data prepared by the nonpartisan Employee Benefit Research Institute (EBRI) shows that over 70 percent of workers earning from $30,000 to $50,000 participated in employer-sponsored retirement plans when a plan was available, whereas less than 5 percent of those middle income earners without access to an employer-sponsored plan contributed to an IRA (see chart #2).[2] In other words, middle class workers are *15 times* more likely to save for their families' retirement at work than on their own.

Because of the effectiveness of these workplace savings opportunities, it is imperative that no harm is done to the current structure of the tax incentives that have motivated employers to voluntarily sponsor and contribute, along with the employees themselves, to these retirement plans. The tax incentive for retirement savings is unique in that it is a deferral, not a permanent exclusion. No income tax is paid on contributions and investment earnings as long as the money stays in the retirement account, but income tax will be paid in the future when benefits are distributed. Also, the tax incentive for employer-sponsored plans, like 401(k) plans, comes with nondiscrimination rules that ensure contributions do not discriminate in favor of highly compensated employees, and limit the amount of compensation that can be included in determining benefits and testing for nondiscrimination. The result is a tax incentive that is more progressive than our progressive income tax system (see chart #3).

Though the current system is working well for millions of American workers, there are ways to adapt the current rules to enhance retirement plan coverage and simplify the current operation of these employer-sponsored plans. With input from its diverse professional national membership, ASPPA has developed a document entitled *Proposals to Enhance the Private Retirement System*[3] which contains more than 30 legislative proposals to improve the current system. These proposals would expand employer-sponsored retirement plan coverage and simplify employer-sponsored retirement plan administration through modest changes to the Internal Revenue Code (IRC) and the Employee Retirement Income Security Act

(ERISA). Fortunately, many of these proposals have already been included into bipartisan and bicameral legislation introduced in the current Congress.

Specifically, the private retirement provisions in Title II of Ranking Member Hatch's Secure Annuities for Employee (SAFE) Retirement Act (S.1270) make numerous sensible reforms. These changes will simplify the operation of employer-sponsored retirement plans by eliminating unnecessary paperwork and traps for the unwary, as well as providing new approaches to expand the availability of workplace savings, especially for small business retirement plans. These common sense proposals will go a long way toward improving the retirement security of millions of working Americans. I commend Ranking Member Hatch for offering these long overdue solutions and applaud your committee's commitment to enhancing the private retirement system and the retirement security of our nation's workers.

I will explain first why the current system should be viewed as a success. Then, I will explain the details of these proposals and why they would make such a positive difference for the American people.

THE CURRENT SYSTEM WORKS

First I would like to review the aggregate amounts of retirement assets accumulated by the American people to date. The numbers are staggering. At the end of 2013, Americans had accumulated more than $23 trillion in retirement assets. Of that amount, $5.9 trillion is held in employer-sponsored defined contribution plans of all types. Another $6.5 trillion is held in IRAs, most of which originated in the form of rollovers from employer-sponsored retirement plans.[4] Make no mistake, however, the single most important factor in determining whether or not workers across the income spectrum save for retirement is whether or not there is a workplace retirement plan. If increasing retirement and financial security is the goal, increasing the availability of workplace savings is the way to get there.

While each person's retirement situation is unique, Fidelity recently conducted a study that aggregated the retirement account balances for clients who had both an investment account through an employer-sponsored retirement plan and an IRA at Fidelity to get a sense of how an average individual participating was performing in the current system. In contrast to reports of "average" 401(k) balances which generally include a wide and disparate variety of age, tenure, and income levels, this study found that for near retirees (ages 55-59), the average combined balance was $328,257.[5] That is a substantial amount of money that these individuals can use, in addition to any social security benefit that these individuals may enjoy, to achieve a secure retirement. This data shows that the retirement system works for those that participate in it over the course of their working careers.

The good news is that over 60 million working Americans currently participate in employer-sponsored retirement plans.[6] Contrary to some reports that suggest only about half of American workers have access to these programs, the Bureau of Labor Statistics (BLS) reports that 78 percent of all full time civilian workers had access to retirement benefits at work, and that 83 percent of those workers participated in these arrangements. While availability and take-up rates are substantially lower for part-time workers, even when they are included in these statistics, BLS found that 68 percent of civilian workers had access to retirement plans, and 80 percent of those participate in the offering. For full time private sector workers, BLS found the access and participation rates are 74 percent and 80 percent respectively, and the access and participation rates for all private-sector workers (including part time) are 64 percent and 76 percent, respectively.[7]

Robust as those results are, alternative research even suggests that these estimates may understate what is actually happening in the workplace. A report from the Social Security Administration, based on an integrated assessment of Census data and W-2 records, found that 72 percent of *all* employees who worked at private companies in 2006 had the ability to participate in a retirement plan, and 80 percent of those participated.[8] This analysis, which provided the ability to look at actual data, rather than rely on respondent self-reporting, indicates that the BLS statistics on availability are probably understated.

It is important to bear in mind the current set of incentives that efficiently encourage such a high level of voluntary sponsorship of these programs. This efficiency is derived in large part from two features that set the retirement savings incentives apart from other individual tax incentives. First, by choosing to defer the receipt of their 401(k) contributions in their current pay, individuals defer – but do not escape – their tax obligations. Every dollar that is excluded from income this year will be included in income in a future year. Unfortunately, that is not reflected in the cash basis measurement of the retirement savings "tax expenditure." In fact, the current accounting methodology may overstate the true cost by over 50 percent.[9] Secondly, nondiscrimination rules for employer-sponsored plans assure the plans do not discriminate in favor of highly compensated employees, and limit the amount of compensation that can be included in determining benefits and testing for nondiscrimination. As a result, this tax incentive is more progressive than the current progressive tax code.

This progressivity can be seen in the accompanying chart (see chart #3), which shows that households with incomes of less than $50,000 pay only about 9 percent of all income taxes, but receive 27 percent of the defined contribution plan tax incentives. Households with less than $100,000 in AGI pay about 28 percent of income taxes, but receive about 49 percent of the defined contribution plan tax incentives. Contrast this distribution to the distribution of tax benefit for capital gains, where about 90 percent of the benefit goes to households earning over $200,000.

This mix of incentives and limits has produced a highly effective voluntary retirement savings structure where these workplace programs exist. And, based on the data cited earlier, we know that middle class workers are *15 times* more likely to save for their families' retirement at work than on their own. The key is to find ways to expand the opportunity to save in the workplace. We know that there are still millions of workers across the country that do not yet have access to an employer-sponsored retirement plan, particularly those employed with small employers. A key policy focus for those looking to expand and enhance the nation's retirement security lies in finding ways to make it easier for employers to sponsor these arrangements that we know to be a success.

That is why provisions like those in Title II of Ranking Member Hatch's SAFE Retirement Act are so important. This legislation directly addresses obstacles that frequently keep employers from sponsoring these arrangements, enhancing the likelihood that more workers will have access to these programs in the workplace. Let me explain how they could make a difference.

What Proposals Would Make the Current System Even Better

Even with the success of our current retirement system, there are significant hurdles facing employers from taking on the work and responsibility of sponsoring retirement plans for their employees. These complexities discourage small business owners from taking advantage of the tax incentives for maintaining a plan, or incorporating features that would make the plan more effective as a savings vehicle for all employees, because of the *significant* red tape, fines and penalties that can accompany even the most basic of these arrangements. Some complications are statutory and some are regulatory. The proposals contained in the ASPPA document and in Title II of Ranking Member Hatch's SAFE Retirement Act (S. 1270) address these complexities and complications.

The Starter 401(k) Plan

The Starter 401(k) Plan proposed in S.1270 would give employers that do not already sponsor a 401(k) plan a less expensive option to provide a substantial retirement benefit for their employees. The plan allows employees to save up to $8,000 per year through the arrangement, which is more than individuals can currently save through an IRA, though less than individuals can save through a traditional 401(k) arrangement at present. While the plan does not require employers to make contributions for their employees, it does provide ERISA protections for participants in the plan.

This proposal would also provide start-up companies, who may be reluctant to commit to make employer contributions a way to offer workers a chance to save in a 401(k) plan that could later be easily amended to a traditional 401(k) plan when the business becomes more stable. The Starter 401(k) Plan recognizes that not only are many workers employed by start-ups, but many owners of these entities have very modest incomes themselves and cannot be burdened with retirement contribution requirements when the business is still in the early stages.

Permit Additional Flexibility in Time to Adopt a Retirement Plan

IRS Revenue Ruling 81-114 provides that a deduction for qualified retirement plan contributions is not allowed for a prior taxable year if the plan is not established by the end of that taxable year. Consequently, in order to make deductible contributions for a taxable year, an employer must formally adopt a new qualified retirement plan by the end of such year (unlike a Simplified Employee Pension (SEP) plan, which can be established as late as the due date of the employer's tax filings with extensions).

Frequently, the employer's profitability for a year will be a major factor in his or her decision to establish a retirement plan. This is especially true for small employers. Reliable information on how the business did in the prior year is often not available until after the close of the employer's taxable year. The provision provided in S. 1270 will allow employers to consider the adoption of a qualified retirement plan, or the addition of non-elective contributions to an existing plan, when the final results of the business for the prior year are available. This flexibility would be instrumental in expanding retirement plan coverage and employer-funded retirement benefits, especially for small businesses. This provision will also place ERISA-covered retirement plans on par with a non-ERISA SEP program.

Interim Amendments

Qualified retirement plans are governed by written documents that must meet certain requirements under the Internal Revenue Code (IRC) to maintain tax-favored status. Revenue Procedure 2007-44, as modified by Rev. Proc. 2008-56 and Rev. Proc. 2012-50, provides staggered dates for plan documents to be submitted to IRS for review as to a plan's qualified status. Individually designed plans are on five-year review cycles, and pre-approved documents are on six-year cycles.

During these cycles, plans must adopt amendments to reflect legislative and regulatory changes to the qualification requirements. Except as provided by law or other guidance, these "interim amendments" must generally be adopted by the due date (including extensions) for filing the income tax return for the taxable year the change is effective. There is no coordination of the due dates of these required "interim amendments" with the cycle for submission of documents to IRS.

S.1270 would eliminate mandatory "interim amendments" which increase the cost and burden of maintaining a plan without any corresponding benefit. The current process is incredibly complicated, with different amendment deadlines that vary based upon the type of amendment and the plan's fiscal year. This can lead to mistakes being made by even the most well-meaning plan sponsors (who are voluntarily providing this benefit). Small plan sponsors in particular are justifiably shocked and surprised when asked to pay thousands of dollars in sanctions when an inadvertent mistake in this amendment cycle is uncovered during an IRS audit. Amendment deadlines coordinated with the plan's 5- or 6-year review cycle would be user friendly and cost-effective. This proposal is a perfect example of a simple and sensible change that would streamline the operation of the plan and remove an unnecessary trap for the unwary, but well-meaning employers who are providing retirement benefits for their employees.

Streamline Plan Testing Requirements

A plan is considered "top heavy" if over 60 percent of the accrued retirement benefits are credited to "key employees." Many small business plans are deemed "top heavy" and, as a result, must provide *all* employees, not just those required to be covered under ERISA, in those defined contribution plans with a contribution of at least 3 percent of compensation. For a defined benefit plan, the requirement is a minimum accrued benefit of 2 percent of pay per year of service, with a 20 percent maximum. Special rules apply to participants covered under both types of plans. It is important to note that plan sponsors are still required to engage in non-discrimination testing in addition to the "top heavy" testing if a plan is considered "top heavy."

Unfortunately, these rules serve as a disincentive for employers to add more participants to the retirement plan, especially employees that ERISA allows to be excluded from participation (employees who have not attained age 21 or who have not completed a year of employment with at least 1000 hours of service). Removing this disincentive could easily be accomplished by excluding employees the statute would have allowed to be excluded from participation in the plan from the 3 percent minimum "top heavy" contribution requirement. S. 1270 does this one better, eliminating this extra testing requirement altogether so the employer would not have to worry about allowing more participants to be added to the plan, while still being subject to normal nondiscrimination testing requirements.

Electronic Delivery of Retirement Plan Information to Participants

Under current Department of Labor (DOL) regulations, retirement plan disclosures to participants and beneficiaries required under ERISA must be provided on paper unless the participant or beneficiary chooses to receive disclosures electronically. (There is an exception for employees that have access to a computer as an integral part of their duties at work, but the exception is proving too limited to be useful.) The result is a lot of wasted paper and business time and expense to provide participants and beneficiaries with notices that are not read. Compounding the challenges, new DOL fee disclosure rules for individual retirement plan participants impose substantial additional paper disclosure documents. Real-world experience suggests that participants and beneficiaries might be more inclined to read these notices if they were provided on a more useful, interactive, and environmentally friendly basis through electronic means.

Plan sponsors and service providers should be permitted to default plan participants and beneficiaries into receiving documents electronically, instead of requiring an affirmative election. This change would still permit participants and beneficiaries the ability to elect to receive paper disclosures. S. 1270 addresses the DOL's outdated regulations by allowing all disclosures to participants and beneficiaries required under the IRC and ERISA to be made available to them electronically. Service providers would be required to provide participants and beneficiaries with an advanced notice describing the electronic delivery process and notifying them of their right to opt out of the electronic delivery of documents and receive paper documents instead.

Consolidation and Simplification of Retirement Plan Notice Requirements

S. 1270 makes multiple improvements to plan administration that provide opportunities to consolidate and simplify the multitudes of retirement plan notices to participants and beneficiaries required under the IRC and ERISA. These reforms serve two main purposes that directly benefit the retirement plan participants. First, consolidating and simplifying all the disparate notices into one main, easy to read document increases the likelihood that the information will be read and understood by the participant. Second, consolidating and simplifying these notices reduces the cost to administer the retirement plans, costs that are largely borne by the participants in the plan.

Specifically, S. 1270 allows certain defined benefit plans and certain defined contribution plans that must provide a notice to participants explaining their right to a Qualified Pre-retirement Survivor Annuity (QPSA) to include this notice as part of the Summary Plan Description (SPD). S. 1270 also directs the Secretaries of Labor and the Treasury to adopt final regulations providing that a retirement plan sponsor or service provider may consolidate two or more of the defined contribution employee notices required under the IRC and/or ERISA either into a single notice or consolidate these employees notices into either the SPD or the Summary of Material Modifications (SMM).

The retirement plan sponsor or service provider can have this flexibility provided that the combined notice, SPD, or SMM includes the required content and is provided within the time required by law.

Another unnecessary notice that I feel should be eliminated is the notice requirement for the 3 percent safe harbor. The safe harbor information is already provided to participants and beneficiaries in the SPD, and since employees receive the contribution whether or not they contribute to the plan, it does not cause participants to change their behavior.

"Open" Multiple Employer Plans (MEPs)

The DOL has in recent years concluded that the employers must have a relationship other than joint sponsorship of an employer-sponsored plan to participate in a "multiple employer plan." This determination has effectively decreased the use of these so-called "open" multiple employer plan arrangements, which had gained favor in the marketplace as an option for small employers to provide retirement benefits to their employees.

In response to the DOL's regulatory action, there have been a number of legislative proposals to explicitly permit the operation of open MEPs in the marketplace. The provision in S. 1270 is, in my view, a good approach that permits open MEPs, while providing safeguards for adopting employers through a designated service provider.

CONCLUSION

The current retirement system works well for the tens of millions of Americans that have access to it and has proven a successful vehicle for individuals to save for their future. The key to continued and expanding success is enacting reforms that will further incent employers to provide a retirement savings vehicle for their employees. The private retirement provisions contained in Ranking Member Hatch's SAFE Retirement Act (S. 1270) are a huge step in the right direction to expanding the availability of retirement savings and removing certain complexities from the current system so business owners and service providers are able to provide a better retirement plan product to participants.

Thank you, and I would be happy to answer any further questions that the Committee may have.

APPENDIX

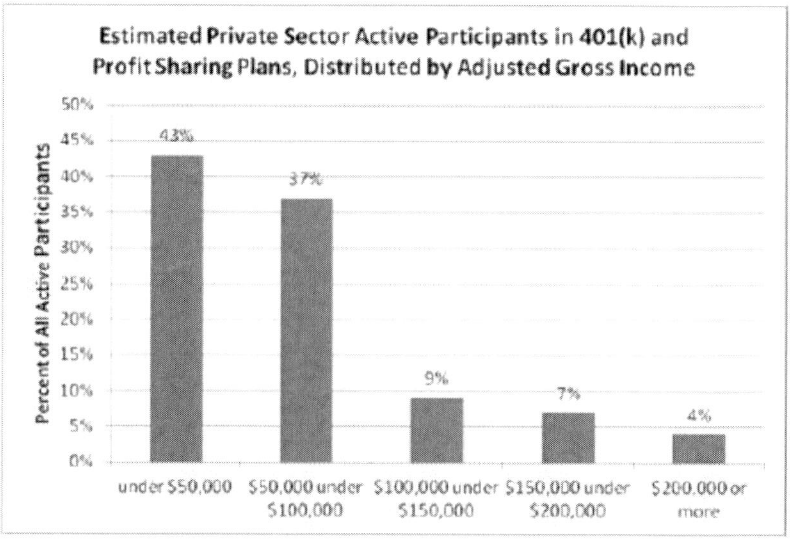

Source: Internal Revenue Service (IRS) Statistics of Income Division (SOI).

Chart #1.

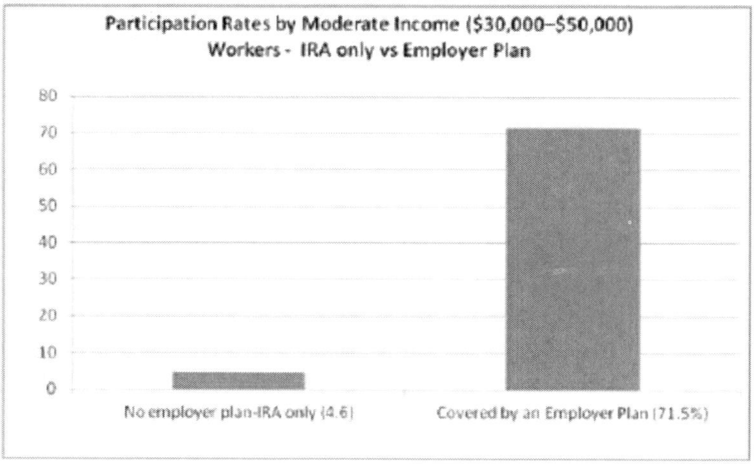

Source: Employee Benefit Research Institute (2010) estimate using 2008 Panel of SIPP (Covered by an Employer Plan) and EBRI estimate (Not Covered by an Employer Plan-IRA only).

Chart #2.

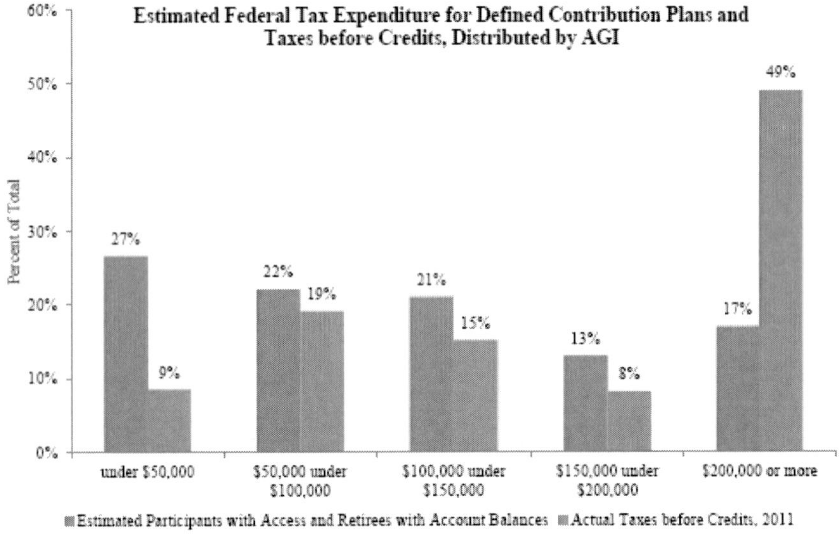

Source: "Distributional Analysis and Pension Tax Provisions", American Society of Pension Professionals and Actuaries (April 2014).

Chart #3.

End Notes

[1] Estimate of private sector active participants in 401(k) and profit sharing plans, distributed by adjusted gross income – Source: Internal Revenue Service, Statistics of Income Division.

[2] Estimate using 2008 Panel of Survey of Income and Program Participation (SIPP) data and 2010 Employee Benefit Research Institute (EBRI) data of workers not covered by an employer plan but saving through an IRA – Source: Employee Benefit Research Institute.

[3] Proposals to Enhance the Private Retirement Plan System (December 2013) – Prepared by the American Society of Pension Professionals & Actuaries Government Affairs Committee.

[4] Investment Company Institute, 2014 Investment Company Fact Book (May, 2014).

[5] Fidelity® Retirement Savings Analysis Highlights Higher Balances and Contribution Rates of Investors Saving Beyond Workplace Savings Plans, (February 28, 2013).

[6] Employee Benefit Research Institute estimates from the March 2013 Current Population Survey.

[7] Bureau of Labor Statistics, Employee Benefits Survey: Retirement Benefits, March 2013: Retirement benefits: access, participation, and take-up rates: National Compensation Survey March 2013.

[8] Irena Dushi, Howard M. Iams, and Jules Lichtenstein, Assessment of Retirement Plan Coverage by Firm Size, Using W-2 Records, Social Security Bulletin (2011).

[9] Judy Xanthopoulos and Mary Schmidt, Retirement Savings and Tax Expenditure Estimates (April, 2012).

In: Individual Retirement Accounts
Editor: Jake Silva
ISBN: 978-1-63482-176-6

Chapter 3

Statement of Ellen E. Schultz, Author and Investigative Reporter. Hearing on "Retirement Savings 2.0: Updating Savings Policy for the Modern Economy"*

Chairman Wyden, Ranking Member Hatch, Members of the Committee, thank you for inviting me.

As a journalist, I have closely followed retirement practices and policy since the later 1980s, for the most part as a reporter and editor at *The Wall Street Journal.* My work has been based largely on my analysis of regulatory filings, internal company memos, and documents that are rarely, if ever, examined by those evaluating the retirement system. And I speak today from that perspective.

You have asked me to comment on whether the tax breaks conferred on retirement plans—expenditures that will likely exceed $100 billion in 2014 – are achieving what Congress intended. Namely, are these costly expenditures helping most working Americans accrue assets adequate to prevent them falling into poverty in their old age and becoming a burden to their families and society?

Based on what I have documented and reported over the past 25 years, that has not been the case. The economic benefits of the tax-subsidies that

* This is an edited, reformatted and augmented version of testimony presented September 16, 2014 before the Senate Finance Committee.

support the retirement system have flowed largely to the highest-paid Americans, to employers, and the financial services industry The expenditures have done too little to improve the likelihood that most of working Americans will have adequate—or any—income (other than Social Security) when they can no longer work.

KEEPING DEFINED BENEFIT PLANS EFFECTIVE

There is no question that defined benefit plans are generally preferable to 401(k) plans and have provided secure and adequate pension benefits to million of people – and they have the potential of providing fair benefits across the board.

Policymakers recognize the value of what defined benefit plans do: Employees are automatically enrolled, professionals manage the investments, and the delayed compensation is ordinarily paid out in retirement as a lifetime annuities that the retiree and spouse cannot outlive.

But over the past two decades, I've seen employers manage their pension plans more for the benefit of the shareholders than the participants, and this committee should explore how to ensure that pension plans continue to be the vehicles envisioned by Congress.

For one thing, employers moved away from the notion that assets in pension plans were essentially locked up for sole purpose of paying benefits to retirees. Among the practices documented in my book, *Retirement Heist*:

- Some employers, including Montgomery Ward, terminated their *healthy* pension plans and used the assets to pay creditors.
- Many, like Verizon, used the assets to finance downsizings, offering departing employees additional pension payouts in lieu of severance.
- Others, including DuPont, used pension assets to pay for retiree health benefits
- In less transparent maneuvers, companies sold pension assets in mergers and acquisitions, indirectly converting pension assets into cash.
- Employers took advantage of tax loopholes to carve out parts of the tax-subsidized pension plans for the rank-and-file to pay for supplemental executive pensions and deferred compensation for highly paid employees. The arrangements are called QSERPs, which

stands for "qualified supplemental executive retirement plans." Using this technique, for example, Intel was able to move more than $200 million in unfunded obligations for deferred compensation for the top 3% to 5% of its workforce into the pension plan. Participants can later roll their QSERP into an IRA.

Employers' ability to treat pension plans like tax-sheltered piggy banks rendered pension plans less well funded, and more likely to fail. It also meant that employers had an incentive to cut pensions and freeze plans –even when the plans were healthy-- because doing so increased the assets available for the employer.

Meanwhile, employers had another incentive to cut pensions: New accounting rules required companies to report pension obligations to shareholders, and their effect on quarterly income. Though intended to increase transparency, the rule had the unintended effect of rewarding companies that cut pension benefits. Doing so generated immediate profits for shareholders, and increased the surplus assets available to the employer.

Another thing to consider when evaluating the effectiveness of tax subsidies for pension plan is that the risk landscape has changed. When ERISA was enacted, employers bore the risk in pension plans (investment, interest rate, mortality) in exchange for the tax subsidies. But employers learned that they can essentially transfer investment and interest rate risk to participants by cutting pension benefits. When pension plans suffered losses, many employers responded by cutting benefits. (Replacing pensions with 401(k)s, of course, transfers *all* risk to the participants). Lump sum payouts are another way to transfer investment and interest rate risk, as well as inflation risk and longevity risk to retirees.

Taking risk transfer even further, a growing number of companies, including General Motors and Verizon, are transferring certain pension obligations to insurance companies, which take over the task of making monthly payments to retirees.

Companies benefit from this "de-risking" strategy, and insurers welcome the assets and fees for managing them, but retirees potentially face solvency risk, because their pensions no longer enjoy the protections of the federal Pension Benefit Guaranty Corp., which steps in to pay pensions if a plan fails.

The concept of "de-risking" requires greater scrutiny to insure there are no replays of 1980s debacles, when companies terminated pension plans and turned the job of paying out pensions to insurers like Executive Life, which became insolvent, causing retirees to lose significant amounts of their pensions.

Even more disturbing, some companies are offering lump sum window "opportunities" to already retired individuals. The lump sum option typically has far less value than the annuity that is already being paid, and many of the people to whom this option is offered are in their late 70s and 80s and some of them will be suffering from diminished capacity. Those who take lump sums are exchanging a secure stream of payments they cannot outlive, and taking on the challenge of investing the money and making it last.

The Effectiveness of Tax Subsidies in 401(k) Plans

With employers freezing and terminating their pensions, and offloading liabilities to insurance companies and individuals, 401(k)-style savings plans have become the primary vehicle for retirement savings. The problem is that although the U.S. Treasury foregoes billions of dollars every year to encourage retirement saving, the workers who most need a supplement to Social Security either get nothing or very little from these plans.

According to the Center for Retirement Research, only about half of private sector workers participate in a workplace retirement plan, and roughly one-third of households reach their sixties with no retirement plans at all.

The reality is that a disproportionate amount of the tax expenditure ends up benefitting affluent employees who are already saving. Two-thirds of the value of tax expenditures for retirement savings plans goes to households in the top income quintile, according to the Urban-Brookings Tax Policy Center.

Many blame low savings rates on the behavior of low and middle income workers: failing to contribute, or contributing too little, making poor investment choices, or cashing out what little they have accumulated to pay for pressing needs like health care, rent, college tuition, and home attendants for their elderly parents.

But there are also other reasons. For example, millions of workers who are excluded altogether from participation in their employer's retirement plans. Although 401(k)s and other retirement plans are supposed to be made available to the broad base of employees, and not just a select group, employers are permitted to exclude 30% of workers for any reason, and even more if they follow certain rules. They can exclude workers in certain divisions, or geographic areas and job classifications. They may also exclude those who work fewer than 1,000 hours in a 12-month period, which can effectively eliminate part-timers and seasonal workers; people under age 21, and workers covered by collective bargaining agreements.

Excluding low-paid workers who are not likely to contribute or contribute very little makes it easier for the retirement plans to pass discrimination tests, which compare the contributions of low-paid to those of high paid, to ensure that the plan doesn't unfairly benefit the top echelon. If too few of the lower paid participate, and contribute too little, a plan can appear discriminatory, which can bring down the maximum amount the high-paid can contribute. One way to ensure that low participation by lower paid workers doesn't make the plan appear discriminatory is to exclude many of them altogether.

One example in my book is Hugo Boss, a company that makes high-end clothing. For years, the company excluded workers in its warehouse in Midway, Georgia, from the 401(k) plan that it offered to the 232 employees and managers at its Cleveland headquarters. Low participation and contributions from the low-paid warehouse workers, mostly minority women, would have cause the plan to fail the discrimination tests. When that happens, the limits on what the highest paid employees can contribute are lower than the statutory maximum, which currently is $17,500 plus a $5,500 catch-up contribution for those 50 and over.

Thus, those who need savings incentives the most are shut out of plans to ensure that those who need help the least can contribute the maximum amount.

A recurring theme I've seen since the '80s is that many employers want to maintain the plans primarily for the benefit of their higher paid employees, and with the help of benefits consulting firms, use increasingly complex maneuvers to sidestep the discrimination rules and skew benefits to the highly paid. These include segregating lower-paid workers in separate but unequal plans, and providing larger contributions to higher-paid workers, a nearly universal practice common in pension plans, called "permitted disparity." Younger and lower-income workers are also more likely to forfeit employer contributions because they don't remain on the job long enough to vest.

Employers have persistently sought relief from discrimination rules, and lobbied successfully for the automatic enrollment provision included in the Pension Protection Act, which become effective in 2007. Although sold as a way to improve participation among the low-paid, who are automatically enrolled in a plan, the benefit to employers is that merely by providing automatic enrollment (even if workers opt out), and making a modest matching contribution to an employee's account, the plans don't have to prove that they are benefiting lower paid employees.

It remains to be seen whether auto-enrollment will provide a meaningful benefit for the low-paid. Employees can drop out at any time, aren't required to contribute, can use the plan as a piggy bank for immediate spending needs, and must work for three years before they vest in the employer contributions. Meanwhile, only *non-excluded* employees are auto-enrolled, and employers can continue to take advantage of "permitted disparity" to provide richer contributions to the highest paid employees in the plans.

LOOKING AHEAD

Using tax breaks as carrots to encourage savings is potentially a good thing , but more scrutiny is needed to determine how to structure them to work more efficiently.

For example, the increase in 401(k) limits in 2001 (and indexed to inflation) has not significantly increased the number of retirement plans or the percentage of people participating. [Currently, the maximum combined employer-employee contribution to a 401(k) is $52,000.]

A rollback of contribution levels, or at least a freeze at the current level might be something to consider. According to the GAO, only a small percentage of workers contribute the maximum to their plans. Contribution ceilings do not jeopardize the ability of more affluent employees to save on a tax deferred basis. Many of the highest paid participate in deferred compensation plans that enable them to save significant amounts above the contribution limits. Savings in these parallel 401(k)s receive employer contributions, can be invested in virtual versions of the same funds available in the 401(k), and enjoy grow tax deferred growth.

In any discussion of tax expenditures, it would be illuminating to measure revenue loss attributable to the billions of dollars that highly paid employees set aside each year in deferred compensation plans and supplemental executive pensions plans, which at some companies exceed the amounts owed regular workers.

And we need more information from employers.

To get a clearer view of who benefits from tax-payer subsidized retirement plans, employers should once again be required to submit Schedule T of the Form 5500, which for each plan shows:

- Total employees
- Total number of excluded workers,
- Number of excluded workers by classification:

  - work fewer than 1,000 hours a year
  - worked less than one year
  - under 21
  - location (excluded division/unit)
  - job category
  - collectively bargained

Total participants in the plan

Number of participants with anything in their accounts

Demographic data would also be helpful when evaluating who benefits from qualified plans. Employers could be required to disclose the race, gender and ages of both participants and excluded employees.

Thanks you for your time. I'd be glad to answer any questions.

INDEX

G

H

I

J

L

M

S

T

U

V

W

Y